AF334127

Advance Reviews

"Like many other single women, I've always assumed that being married and having tons of money would make life so much easier. Reading Rebecca Reese's book *I'm Married to a Millionaire, So Why Am I In Therapy?* shattered those myths for me and gave me confidence that I'm on the right track in being committed to finding inner peace, happiness, and purpose so I can be fully present to life as it is and eventually attract the right man for me instead of hiding behind my career. This isn't a dating book, but Rebecca shares her journey of self-discovery that helped her step into happiness and purpose in her life beyond her marriage and family, and it speaks to the soul of women everywhere (regardless of your financial or marital status). It's truly a story of a journey that must begin from within, and it's a message that all women need to read."

~ **Lisa Manyon**, Write On Creative, www.writeoncreative.com

"I was blown away by the honesty and depth of feeling Becky Reese reveals in *I'm Married to a Millionaire, So Why Am I In Therapy?* Her story is a stark reminder that we cannot look outside ourselves for the love, security, and happiness we crave so much. The journey starts and ends within."

~ **JJ Virgin**, PhD, CNS, Nutrition & Fitness Expert, www.jjvirgin.com

"A sheer gem of hope and renewal for every woman's spirit! Becky's authenticity and candid story-telling poignantly show us what's possible when we surrender to learning how to love ourselves from the inside out."

~ **Kendall Summerhawk**, Million Dollar Marketing Coach and Co-founder of the IAWBC, International Association of Women in Business Coaching, www.kendallsummerhawk.com

"Don't be misled into thinking that if you're not a millionaire or in therapy this book is not for you. On the contrary, each of us can relate to Becky Reese because we're all taught by society to seek meaning by accumulating more, more, more. It takes guts to reveal to the world your deepest fears and greatest flaws. But Becky holds nothing back, and because of that, her story reminds us that no amount of outward success will fulfill us until we first discover how to love ourselves. Thanks, Becky, for sharing yourself with us."

~ **Angelique Rewers**, ABC, APR, The Corporate Agent,
   www.bonmotcomms.com

"This is a book I did not want to put down, even for a second. It is truly one of the best written self-help books I have ever read. Becky stepped up to the plate to expose herself and her frailties to the world and, as a result, will be able to help everyone who reads her book in ways they've never imagined."

~ **Patricia Noel Drain**, Author, Speaker, Mentor,
   www.PatriciaDrain.com

"When you read this book, you will be all at once inspired, and taken on an incredible emotional journey that culminates with the ultimate life lesson: learning to love yourself."

~ **Dallas Travers**, CEC, The Tao of Show Business,
   www.DallasTravers.com

"Becky Reese, shares more in her book than most women would dare to bare! Brave, insightful, profound, and inspiring. A must-read for any women who is feeling lost and alone. Reese will make you rethink how you feel about yourself, how you take care of your spirit and soul, and what you truly value in your life. This book will change how you see yourself, make you realize you have unlimited potential, and confirm the fact that having money isn't the answer to living a full and meaningful life. Not everyone has the strength Reese does to be so candid. She transforms her life, and her book will help many others do the same."

~ **Tamara Gold**, *The Art of Beautiful*, www.TamaraGold.com

"Moms everywhere need to read this book! Not only is it an excellent resource for them but for young women, too. This book illuminates the fact that women are powerful beings, but the details of everyday life have a way of making us forget that when we don't pay attention to ourselves. A touching and inspirational story!"

~ **Sheri McConnell**, CEO/Business Model Expert, Smart Women's Institute of Entrepreneurial Learning, www.smartwomeninstitute.com

"I loved reading Becky Reese's impressive and inspirational book, *I'm Married to a Millionaire, So Why Am I In Therapy?* I felt like a close confidante as she shared her honest stories of the loss of her sister, a baby and almost, herself. A wonderful mom of five, a marathon runner and wife of a savvy and successful man, Becky reminds us that we are all works-in-progress. Sometimes we have to hit bottom, before we have the courage to say 'Enough!' and carve out some precious time for ourselves on the path to a life of joy, beauty, fulfillment and love. Becky empowers women and gives them permission to be themselves without guilt. Amen, sister!"

~ **Susan Mathison**, MD, *Positively Beautiful*, www.PositivelyBeautiful.com

"How refreshing to experience such a candid, compelling and inspiring tale of one woman's journey to find meaning in her life. I applaud Ms. Reese for her honesty and truth. Her story serves as a beacon to other women. May her words guide them to their own paths of discovery. Bravo!"

~ **Alexa Fischer**, *Lessons For the Limelight*, www.AlexaFischer.com

I'm Married to a Millionaire,

So Why am I in Therapy?

Life is how you live it,
Not how you spend it!

Rebecca Reese

with Amy Gregory Spence

DEDICATION

It is with boundless love that I dedicate this book to my husband Mike. You have encouraged and supported me on every step of this journey! When I cried as I struggled to share painful memories, you reminded me how proud you and the kids are of me. When I wanted to quit, you reminded me why I needed to finish. Thank you. I love you.

To my children. Thank you for understanding all of the time I had to spend away from you to finish this book. You are the light in my life. I love being a mom, and I will love you all always, and forever.

To my Mom and Dad. You are amazing parents, and I am so grateful to you both for all your love and support. Thank you for everything. I love you always.

Lastly, to everyone who has inspired me along this journey, I am honored and blessed by your encouragement and support. You have helped me live my dream. For those of you who worked with me during the editorial process, I thank you for your guidance and your patience!

And now, thanks to all of you, I am able to fulfill another dream! You are helping create Reese Children's Charities, specifically the Harry and Sally Eick College Scholarship. I cannot think of a better way to honor both my parents and my husband, than to create a legacy in their names!

To those of you who have purchased the book, I truly hope you will find some wisdom and enlightenment within these pages that will translate into some good in your life. I know God is with you, showing you the way.

I'm Married to a Millionaire, So Why am I in Therapy?
Life is how you live it, Not how you spend it!
Rebecca Reese

ISBN: 978-1-936214-48-8
Library of Congress Control Number: 2011930653

Published by Copper Leaf Publishing, LLC
A Wyatt-MacKenzie Imprint

marriedtoamillionairebook.com
BeckyReese.com

©2011 Rebecca Reese

All rights reserved.

No part of this book may be used or reproduced in any manner whatsoever without written permission of the editor/copyright owner except in the case of brief quotations embodied in articles or reviews.

Smartly published™ through the

Smart Women's Institute
of Entrepreneurial Learning
Imprint Publishing Program

in collaboration with

Wyatt-MacKenzie Publishing
DEADWOOD, OREGON

Contents

1
Learning How to Water the Grass

"The bad news is the past was in your hands, but the good news is that the future, my friend, is also in your hands."

~ ANDY ANDREWS

$\mathcal{W}$e all have moments when we are frustrated with life. When we realize we are absolutely miserable. When we realize that we are still stuck in a place of fear, depression, and loneliness. For me, though, it didn't make any sense.

Some time ago, I was driving and felt angry at the way my life was working. In the big picture, I knew it was ridiculous because I had money. Lots of it. I could buy what I wanted, drive what I wanted, and vacation where I wanted. I should have been happy. Right? But I wasn't.

I pulled over to the side of the road, whipped out my iPhone, and starting typing out a list of things that were bothering me. (I envisioned my therapist gleaming with pride at my attempt to sort out my feelings.) My fingers maniacally flew over the keyboard trying to make some sense out of the swirl of emotions and jumbled thoughts that were scattered across my mind. I named the list "What I Hate" and wrote...

1) My waistband. Specifically, tight waistbands. I hated the crushing force with which they gripped my midsection. They made me uncomfortable. They ungraciously pointed out that I was a big girl in a size 0 world. They screamed, "See, you may have more cash in your wallet than other people, but you still don't fit in. You'll always be too big."

2) Mail. I hated getting it because it reminded me of the hard times—the mailbox bulging with threatening letters from bill collectors, lawsuit documents, and unpaid invoices. I didn't want to go back to the financially unstable place where my husband and I had started out.

3) Friends. That was an easy one. I had none. But I did have plenty of people whom I let take advantage of me. Unconsciously, I pimped myself out like an ATM. Money had ruined many relationships and made me suspicious of other people's intentions. I'm sure you've heard the warning not to lend money to family or friends. Right? Well, I ignored that sound advice many times, and many times the end result turned into a worst case scenario. People dropped out of the picture after I loaned them money. Loans were never repaid. Friends felt entitled to a piece of my pie and kept asking for more of my pie. Consequently, I became bitter and angry. But hey, what am I complaining about? I opened my wallet, whipped out my checkbook, and thrust out my credit card whenever the restaurant/car/clothing/medical bill needed to be paid to whomever. What I got in return was superficial relationships, broken friendships, and a life of loneliness where I didn't trust anyone.

4) Life stress. People assume money eliminates stress, even the normal stress that comes when you bring five children into the world. This is not true. When you make more money, you get bigger bills. And family life is pretty much the same. Kids get sick. They need to be shuffled from here to there. Meals need to be prepared. Rooms need to be cleaned. Conflicts with family and friends happen. I had hoped that being financially secure meant I'd have a butler and a cute pool boy and be able to sunbathe all day with a piña colada in my hand while Mary Poppins took care of my children. Yeah, not so much.

5) Lack of self-control. While my kids ran around the house making messes, chasing dogs and crying about something, I tried to prove how great I was and worked at being a "good" eater, staying away from supersized portions and junk food. No such luck. Maybe this is a woman thing. There were countless times when I didn't know how to say no to food. I ate when I wasn't hungry, ate too much when I was, and I even hoarded food. I would buy a chocolate cake, pretending it was for the kids (don't judge me; I'm sure you have done the same thing at least once), and ate it later by myself. I didn't have any friends so I befriended the refrigerator. Embarrassing.

I know, I know. You might be thinking, "Would you like some cheese with that whine?" But that's just how I felt. It was what it was. On that day—pulled over on the shoulder of Highway such-and-such—sure, I fumed and pouted and aired all my frustration on the list. Here's the thing, it was also the day I had an epiphany. The moment didn't end with my laundry list of complaints. After all, life is all about perspective, right?

As cars whizzed by, suddenly my fingers froze. I stopped typing. Instead of bellyaching about my life, I started asking questions. Deep ones. Soul-searching ones. Ones that dug into the core of my being. What is true happiness? How do I get rid of my angst? How can I live better?

My perspective shifted a second time when I started thinking about stuff that I wanted. Good stuff. Real stuff. Stuff like love, approval, acceptance, feeling comfortable in my own skin, loving me. Not I-want-Jessica-Simpson's-hair or a-day-at-the-spa kind of stuff. Then I got to the best part of my epiphany. The final turn. I wrote down that everything is going to be okay.

Everything. Is. Going. To. Be. Okay.

Maybe you would have gotten to that nugget of wisdom a little sooner than I did, but it took writing a list for me to get to that place. And it happened right after the time in my life when I had made a decision to take care of myself mentally, emotionally, and spiritually for the first time in eighteen years. By the end of 2009, I was starting to live again. But my resurrection certainly didn't happen overnight. It took a string of events to lead me to the transformation that would help reclaim my identity and redefine my purpose.

Writing my list was one such event. It served as a reminder that things would work themselves out in my life if I continued to focus on what is important like my inner well-being. I still have that list with me. I look at it daily and it helps me remember that happiness and contentment are not found in circumstances or stuff; it's an inside job.

Recently I read Geneen Roth's book *Women, Food and God*. I've always loved her as an author and have appreciated her powerful insights into the battle women have with food and their bodies. And I, like a lot of women, can relate to the inner war of being unhappy in life because this diet failed, or those pants don't fit anymore, or feeling miserable because I can't fit into my pre-pregnancy jeans.

So many of us base our level of happiness and contentment on what we look like or—here's a big one—how much money we have. I can tell you that I have experience in both areas. In an article entitled, "Love the One You're With", Geenen wrote, "All we ever have is now. If you can't look around now and see the abundance in your life, you won't be able to notice it in five years either, no matter how thin you are. Happiness is not about changing your circumstances but changing the eyes through which you view your circumstances." See? Perspective.

In my life, there was one area where my circumstances were settled and looked pretty good on the outside. It was a place where I didn't have to worry about not having enough. A place where I didn't have to be concerned about where I would get money to pay the bills next month. A place where going on vacation and affording luxury items were not things I had to carefully calculate into my budget. I didn't even have a budget.

I was the wife of a millionaire. My husband and I worked hard, made wise investments, and climbed the ladder of success that led us to a place of financial stability and a little beyond. So I should have been happy, right? Well, friend, in many ways I was. I was definitely grateful for that security, especially because financial stress is the number one reason many couples divorce. It's hard not having money. I get it. When my husband and I started out, we barely survived from paycheck to paycheck.

I understand that in many cases, money does make the

world go 'round. In this day and age, we can't live without it. Can't live in a house without paying a mortgage, utilities, and the whole shebang; need money for that. Can't get to work without gas in your car; need money for that. Can't feed your babies without buying food; need money for that.

The other side of the coin is just as true. Money doesn't solve everything. Money doesn't make you beautiful. Money doesn't create a solid marriage. Money doesn't give you self-worth. Money doesn't hug you, love you, inspire you, bring you peace, or comfort you in the long run.

Before my transformation, I was living a good life as far as my financial statements, but on the inside I was crumbling like a sugar cube. I was living on the edge of stress. For the last eighteen years, my world consisted of caring for my husband and our five children and helping out with our multiple businesses. It was a routine I had mastered well. Take care of everyone else and forget about me. As I struggled to create a constant peaceful environment for my family, a deep sea was raging inside of me.

My people-pleasing skills were as sharp as a razor. I was an over-achiever when it came to making everyone around me happy. I did a thorough job not taking care of myself. I didn't know how to take care of myself. I didn't think I deserved to take a break and indulge in a fifteen-minute bubble bath. Though I was an avid runner, I was gaining weight. I was disappearing into a shell of the woman I had been in my early twenties.

I bought shoes I never wore. I bought clothes I never wore. I bought jewelry I never wore. I had nice cars. I had a big house and a beautiful vacation home. But I was miserable. I allowed food, fear, stress, and anxiety to sabotage my mental, emotional, and even my spiritual health to the point where my nutritionist had a little intervention with me. And that's when

I started to change.

One day I met my nutritionist at her office. I was used to the drill. Sit there for a while and discuss my eating habits (yawn!). Most of our meetings were more draining than anything else. At 5'10" and a size 16, I was stuck at the same weight for a long time. I couldn't seem to free myself from the weight pest nipping at my sore and bruised ankles. I was on the verge of giving up. What did I have to do? I wondered. Starve myself? Chain myself to my bed to avoid trips to the kitchen? Sew my mouth shut?

Though a patient woman, that day I could tell my nutritionist was a bit frustrated with me. With kindness and sincerity in her voice, forced to some extent I'm sure, she said, "Becky, I want you to see a therapist." I felt like a defiant child. My insides burst out into a silent tantrum, even though I calmly took the card from her hand and showed no outward signs of resistance. The adult and mature woman in me expressed appreciation and told her, "Okay, thank you for the recommendation. I think it's a good one." The defiant child in me, however, threw herself on the ground, arms and legs flailing all over the place like a fish out of water, and said, "Whatever, Missy. Just 'cause I've got the card in my hand doesn't mean I'm going. No way, Jose."

I drove home that day clasping the business card and rolling it around my fingers. Therapy? Therapy is for crazy people. People with real problems. People who have been through a traumatic event. Not me. I probably just need a happy pill. Or maybe I just needed someone to get in my face and slap me silly with a reality check.

I decided I'd wait it out. I'd give myself more time to become happy. Normal. Adjusted. Better. After all, no one I knew was in therapy. Granted, I lived in a small town where everyone knows your name, but not one person in the area ever divulged their secret of having sat on a comfy leather couch pontificating upon their life with a professional who charged two hundred bucks an hour. Therapy? Definitely not for me...or so I thought. Deep down inside, I'm sure I felt desperate; I'd do anything to lose weight.

Just before my 39th birthday, in the fall of 2009, I found myself driving to Dr. Sandy McDonald's office for my first therapist appointment. So much for waiting it out, right? I was nervous. When I parked my car in front of the building on a fairly busy street, the butterflies in my stomach started working overtime. I didn't want anyone to see me. I felt like a kid sneaking into a candy shop to shoplift some Tootsie Rolls.

As I stepped out of my car and took the few steps toward the office door, from the corner of my eye I caught a glimpse of a woman I recognized. She was taking her own steps toward her office, which just happened to be next door to Dr. McDonald. What unfortunate timing. I tried to avert my eyes and subtly shift my body away from her direction, but my avoidance strategies failed.

"Hey, Becky," she called out cheerfully. "How are you?" This sweet woman worked as an attorney and used to rent a piece of property from my husband and me. "Hi Mary, I'm good, and you?" We chitchatted for a bit, and I cut our small talk short so I wouldn't miss my appointment. Good lord, I thought. There she was going to work and there I was, about to get my head checked by a shrink. We parted ways and I walked over to Dr. McDonald's office. I mentally prepared myself as best as I could for the hour that would ultimately change the course of my life.

Someone once told me that when you walk into a therapist's office, the first thing you should look for is Kleenex. My therapist's office was stocked. It was well-needed. I sat on her couch for one hour while tears streamed down my face; it was my first time, after all. Sometimes the tears fell gently and quietly. Other times they were torrential and accompanied by heaving sobs and trembling shoulders.

Dr. Sandy McDonald was a beautiful woman. I find it so rare for a woman to be both stunning and brilliant. She had that remarkable coupling, plus she was exceptionally sweet and down to earth. She didn't barrage me with psychobabble or allow her professional status to create an impenetrable wall between patient and doctor, although I recognize boundaries are necessary in this profession.

I have to be honest. A part of me felt this whole thing was quite ridiculous. As I bawled my way through sixty minutes of my new therapist's day, I felt silly for complaining about my life. Why was I even there? I had just bought a car for $100,000, which was probably more money than the blonde doctor in front of me made in two years. I was living the good life. Frankly, I felt guilty for taking up her valuable time and even wasting her trashcan space as my used tissues piled up like Mount Everest.

But Dr. McDonald didn't judge me. She didn't roll her eyes. She didn't tell me to stop being so dramatic and appreciate what I have. She listened. And that was exactly what I needed. The fact was, I was lonely. My sister, my one confidant and best friend in the world, had recently died at the age of 51 from a heart attack. When she died, she took a piece of my heart with her. I felt more than loss. I felt the painful realization that I didn't have any friends. Not the real kind, at least. It's hard to find genuine people in the fast life. Most people want something from you. I didn't. I just wanted a friend.

I spewed out stuff that had been boiling inside, stuff that I was never able to talk about with anyone because I had been so guarded. Dr. McDonald was clearly a godsend. When I left her office that day, I felt like a whole new world had opened for me. I was changing. I was growing. I had finally taken a step forward into places I had never dared go before.

∞

My first fashion coach, Shari, also fired up my transformation process. I met her after I started therapy. I must admit, it was only through therapy that I could change the way I associated myself with style.

I met Shari at a conference in Grand Rapids, about two and a half hours from where I live. An organization called "Hearts at Home" held the conference. I had heard good things about it so I was anxious to go. But I was also a little hesitant because I'd have to share a room and one bathroom with three women I didn't know. I wasn't anti-social or a snob. Far from it. I just didn't know these women. I had been so hurt by strangers and close friends in the past that a part of me preferred my own company. It was easier that way. Even though I went to the conference, I checked myself into a different hotel.

When I looked at my conference itinerary and discovered I didn't get into Shari's workshop, my heart sank. It was the one segment I wanted to hear because I knew I needed it. I was desperate. I was determined to go, whether or not I was on the roster. I know, I know. I'm such a workshop-crashing rebel. Someone should have called the Christian women's conference cops on me.

When I walked into the breakout room that afternoon, I was surprised to see I wasn't the only sneaky person at this conference. The room was packed with women whom I knew for a fact had not signed up for the class. Shari was that good. Everyone wanted to hear what she had to say.

Shari has an unmistakable presence on and off stage. I

watched this striking woman begin her presentation and I was immediately transfixed. She was tall, all long arms and legs and she had red hair, not an obnoxious shade but a hue that flattered her ivory, smooth complexion. As she flitted across the stage, her outfit seemed to dance and conform to her body with every move. Her breezy pants and silky tunic looked like it cost her firstborn. I was impressed, but not just because of how she looked.

For two hours, I learned about how to dress for my body shape, not just to make me look skinny but to balance my particular shape. I learned about what colors would flatter me and what colors—some of which I was even sporting at the time—would make me look tired, sluggish, and spent. I learned how to accessorize my outfit so I looked put-together, not like a walking cheap tween jewelry store.

I knew I had to meet Shari one-on-one. But more than that, I knew she had to help me. That was it. I decided she was going to me get out of my sweatpants and sweatshirt rut. After she ended her workshop and the applause thundered throughout the room, she gracefully sauntered to the back of the room. Immediately, she was swarmed with women. I was patient. I stayed a while. When I finally had the chance to introduce myself and ask her to be my personal fashion coach, she seemed thrilled. Her green eyes genuinely sparkled and her smile was inviting. Her manicured hand flashed an enormous statement ring. She placed that hand on my shoulder and she said she would be delighted to talk further after the conference.

This is why I needed her so desperately. When you become a part of a particular social circle—and it doesn't have to be the rich-and-famous club; it can just as easily be a clique of fashionista moms in your hip neighborhood—you start to notice some things. People dress differently. More specifically, they dress better than you. They don't drop their kids off at school or run to the grocery store wearing sweatpants and tennis shoes.

When they step out of their houses, they look like high-end fashion models in a couture magazine, even if they are only picking up a gallon of milk. When they go to dinner, dressing up takes on a whole new meaning. They drape themselves in exquisite fashion and showcase huge, shiny baubles that cost more than the average family car. They wear five-inch heels that have labels slapped on them of designers whose names I still need help pronouncing. Oh, and they definitely don't wear mom jeans.

Please don't misunderstand me. I'm not speaking badly of women who do a great job keeping up their appearances by dressing well and taking care of their bodies. We all have a right to feel good about ourselves. Part of that can mean making wise healthy choices and learning how to match, accessorize, and wear the right colors.

When my husband started mingling with the upper crust and we found ourselves going to this event and that dinner and this country club and that summer home, I quickly realized I didn't fit in. The challenge for me was that I was not used to dressing, as I like to say, on purpose. I was used to putting on the cleanest, most comfortable, and most accessible outfit I could find before waking up the kids and rushing down the stairs to make breakfast, get them ready for school, and do a little housecleaning. Stepping out of the house at seven in the morning with my hair done, makeup on, and wearing a cute tracksuit with something glittery on it were tasks that were way out of my league.

Needless to say, the pressure was on. I didn't want to change who I was, I just wanted to feel good about myself. It was a hard balance to achieve.

Enter Shari. I did my spring shopping with her in Miami. We flew to Florida together and as soon as we shuttled ourselves in and out of an endless array of clothing stores, the tension was obvious. We were in the throes of a fashion tug of war, though we were both as polite as could be to the other.

Whenever I chose a blouse or a pair of pants I liked and thought would look good on me, Shari shook her head. We went through this cycle numerous times. "How 'bout this one?" I said as I held up a pastel top on a hanger and jiggled it in Shari's direction. It was a beautiful shade of pink and seemed to hug the right curves; at least it did on the mannequin in the front window.

Shari cocked her head to one side and quickly shook her head like a maraca. Her "no" rang loud and clear. Again. "I have something better for you, though," she announced. Her dangly earrings glowed like a firelight as it caught the Miami sun's rays in the window. She held up an orange, short-sleeved, linen blazer. It reminded me of something my sixty-year-old aunt would wear.

I gulped and thought, "So not for me."

I love fashion magazines and couture catalogs. I flip through them all the time. I like what I see and I see myself decked out in those clothes. I want to wear the Alberta Ferretti ruffled chiffon-front dress. I want to wear Dolce & Gabbana's velvet back leopard dress. I want to wear the Pucci top with the feathers. But when you are my size, stuffing yourself into something made for a size 6 and under makes you look pudgy and fat.

Shari knew that, but I wasn't happy with her alternatives. When she showed me something that would flatter my figure, I immediately thought it belonged in the clothing section for grandmothers. Maybe my thoughts were a bit extreme but still, I didn't want to wear a denim jacket that looked like it had been

Bedazzled and belonged at a Kentucky county fair. I wanted to wear something a size 2 Armani model would wear.

Shari proposed outfit after outfit. I gulped in horror each time. Hours passed and we were both getting tired. We took a break and headed to Starbucks. I didn't say much on the way because I was tired and frustrated and I felt like this was a wasted trip. I thought perhaps I had pegged Shari wrong. Maybe she wasn't as good as I thought. Or maybe, just maybe, it was me.

Suddenly it hit me. Like a hammer on an anvil, I was struck by this epiphany: I wanted to feel sexy in my own way. I didn't necessarily want to look like the perfectly-dressed-manicured-bodied-and-designer-outfitted women that swarm-ed the sidewalks of South Beach, but I didn't want to feel dowdy either. I wanted to feel like a hot goddess in a way that was all Becky Reese.

I continued to shop with Shari the rest of the day and took home some outfits which I never wore and useful pointers that helped forge the path to finding my own style. Not long after that meeting I met Tamara, my current coach who is much more than a stylist. She didn't just drape me with fancy blouses or dresses in flattering colors; she made me dig deep into my spirit and excavate my authentic self. She forced me to confront my sexy self that was stuck in frump. She taught me how to bring out the inner vixen not just by wearing gorgeous clothes but by attitude and confidence. Tamara helped bring me to the real Becky Reese. She helped guide me to the final stop where I was finally able to reconcile my inner and outer sexiness.

Here's the skinny. There is no material object or physical characteristic that can make you feel perfect, worthy, or good enough. Money. Beauty. Success. Cars. Fame. Fortune. Prestige. A cool job. None of these things afford peace, joy, and happiness. Sure, they can make you feel temporarily good and can enhance your life to a degree, but they are nothing more than material things that can fade just as fast as the hype behind the new Hollywood It Girl.

I've learned how to live a fulfilling and meaningful life by enjoying every day and learning how to be kind to myself. It wasn't easy. It took a long time. I realized it was time to work on the inner Becky Reese and begin the journey to embracing myself, my body, my lifestyle, and discovering what makes me happy. I realized I had a lot of growing to do.

I had a big misconception about money. When my husband and I got married and struggled to pay our bills, I thought if we had more money, most of our problems would be solved. Life would be better. I would feel happier. Less stressed. More purposeful. I definitely appreciate the lifestyle I get to enjoy, but I've learned a fundamental truth.

If you believe the grass is greener on the other side, you're right...but only if you are prepared to fertilize and water it.

2
Building Blocks

"It happens to everyone as they grow up. You find out who you are and what you want, and then you realize that people you've known forever don't see things the way you do.
So you keep the wonderful memories, but find yourself moving on."
~ Nicolas Sparks

My brother and I sat at the bottom of the staircase, our knobby knees knocking together. We had to stay put for who-knew-how-long. While we sat in silence, a noise filled the house that screamed bloody murder. The deafening wail was coming from our mother's bedroom. It was one of many incidences where she would cry out for hours in sheer agony. She suffered from depression and this was one way the disease actualized itself.

I looked at my brother and said, "Mom's sad again." He nodded. By now we were familiar with the routine—sit tight and don't move until the storm blows over. For hours, we would wait on the step for our father to get home, taking a break only if we had to go potty. Dad had the magic touch. He could usually calm Mom down enough for my brother and me to return to our toys and books or whatever we were doing before her outburst.

Though only six years old, I was used to the screaming. Well, I was used to the fact that it happened a lot, not used to the actual screaming; the screaming scared the living daylights out of me. There were three "safe" places in the house where I would hide when my mom's fits erupted. If I was with my brother Andy, we'd sit on the staircase. Otherwise, I'd take refuge behind the living room couch or by the baseboard heater in the family room. I'd close my eyes real tight and pray Daddy would get home sooner than later. I'd pray that I could somehow tune out the piercing cries.

My mother spent a good portion of her day in bed. On several occasions she had to be taken to the hospital because her back would hurt from lying on it so much. She was eventually diagnosed as a manic-depressive. I now know that my mom had been mentally sick since she was a young adult. Depression wasn't a hot topic back in that day and it certainly wasn't a "socially acceptable" disorder. Our family tucked the issue away under the proverbial rug. We didn't address it. We didn't talk about it. To this day, the episodes are understood to be a don't-go-there topic. Maybe it was too painful. I know for me it still is.

Mom's mental instability created in me a deep fear. Not fear of her, but of what could trigger her crying explosions. I felt like I had to walk on eggshells all the time because the last thing I wanted was to be the catalyst for her episodes. I was petrified that if I practiced the piano wrong, got a bad grade, didn't eat my vegetables, or wore the wrong pair of socks, I'd set her off and force her to retreat to her room, screaming every step of the way.

I lived in constant fear. Fear that I would be the bad girl that would make my mom upset and ruin everyone's day. Fear that I couldn't make my mom happy. Fear that I couldn't please her. I was burdened by thinking it was my responsibility to create a home atmosphere of peace, of happiness, of calm. It was too much weight for any little girl to carry, and as I became an adult, those same feelings trailed behind me.

My father did his best to comfort me and not let my mom's self-destructive behavior affect me. He would always remind me, "Be patient with your mom. She's really sick"; but I knew it bothered him, too. Many times I overheard him say he prayed that she would stay alive until I graduated kindergarten.

Dad took over when my mother couldn't perform her maternal duties. He played the role of Mr. Mom rather well. He taught me how to eat with a fork, brush my teeth, and tie my shoes. He was an amazing dad. I am and will forever be grateful to him for all he taught me.

As a kid, I never understood exactly what he meant by "sick". I assumed it meant my mother was in some kind of pain; maybe her tummy or head hurt. Or maybe she cried so much because she was very sad.

I hated the emotional outbursts. They scared me. Sometimes she was so loud, we were afraid the neighbors would call the cops, thinking something bad was happening either to her or to one of us.

I was afraid that I would see policemen at our door or hear sirens from an ambulance that might screech to a stop in front of our house and take Mom away. I was humiliated to be the spectacle on the block, to watch nosy neighbors line up outside their houses to catch a glimpse of the madness.

My sister Carol was sixteen years my senior. We became close in my adult years and frequently talked about the different childhoods we had. She remembered traveling extensively all over the world and even living in Sweden for a long period of time. At that time, our mom was happy, fun, and energetic—sides of her I rarely saw. Carol spent little time with my dad because he worked long hours, unlike me who spent most of my early years being raised by him. When my sister went off to college a few years after I was born, my mom checked out; her episodes came on full-force.

Truthfully, the pain I endured from living with a mother tormented by mental illness made me very suspicious of people. I expected inconsistency. I expected instability. I was even uncomfortable being in an environment of peace and calm because those two elements were foreign to me. I feel I was cheated out of having a mother. Though Mom has amazing qualities, I still cannot escape the reality of her absence for most of my crucial growing up years.

Many people didn't see the manic side of my mom and when the illness was dormant, she was an involved and engaging parent. Both Mom and Dad came to all of our track meets, basketball games, soccer practices, and any other activity. Mom also loved to cook. Okay, maybe not loved, but she learned to with eight kids. We never went out to eat; we didn't need to. She would hole herself up in the kitchen and whip up a homemade pie or pizza. She also loved books and would read the classics to us every night before bed.

Life wasn't all bad. Other than my mother's manic-depressive outbreaks, my childhood was pretty uneventful. Born and raised in East Lansing, Michigan, I was the youngest of eight children: six boys, John, Steve, Tim, Chris, Peter, and Andy, and two girls, my sister Carol and me. I was born on October 15, 1970, and by the time I was old enough to know my sister, she was off to college. At home I was the princess, the proverbial and literal baby of the family, surrounded by six boys. As protected and adored as they made me feel, my brothers also did a good job of turning me into a little tomboy.

For as long as I can remember, I've been going to football and basketball games. I've been around motorcycles and underneath the hood of many different kinds of clunkers my brothers were always fixing. I was mowing lawns before I knew how to shave my legs and could outrun any girl in my class with the speed I perfected trying to beat my brothers at countless games of tag.

As the baby, I grew up sheltered and protected. When I got old enough to start dating, just seeing a glimpse of my towering 6'5" brothers would send any boy in my school running as far away from me as possible. Nobody wanted to risk vying for my attention when I had a six-man security team in my family; only a few were brave enough to try.

Our town was home to Michigan State University where my dad was a chemistry professor. Because of what he did for a living, I was introduced to computers earlier than most of the kids my age. I'd hang out with him at the lab whenever I didn't have to go to school and he would teach me about email and other things.

The lab was a creative utopia. I played on, what seemed to me as a little girl, a huge computer. I satisfied my hungry curiosity by conducting experiments like makeshift volcanoes set up by my dad. I wrote notes and drew on the large chalkboard that took up an entire wall and marveled at the massive piles of important looking books that were stacked everywhere.

My best memories growing up were autumn and winter Sundays and the summers. On those chilly Sundays, my mom would do the laundry and my dad would build a fire where all the boys would gather near and watch football. I'd take my afternoon nap on the cozy rug in front of the cackling flames and would wake up with warm laundry piled around me, courtesy of my mom.

During the winters, I'd curl up in front of the fireplace and gaze outside our big family room window at the picturesque setting. It seems to snow all the time in Michigan. Almost every day I got to stare at a breathtaking view of a winter wonderland; snow adorned the naked branches and covered the ground with its glistening and pure white beauty.

Summers were spent at our cottage in Traverse City, about three hours away from home. A former sleepy lumber town, Traverse City is now a famous sporting and resort area. Surrounded by dense forests and miles and miles of sugar sand beaches, this small town is rich in culture and history. Cute, colorful cottages dot the downtown area and bring a gingerbread ambiance to the otherwise bustling historic district. A few steps from the main drag is one of many beaches along the shiny blue and clear waters. Only a few miles away, lush forests line the roadways with a never-ending blanket of evergreen and pine trees.

Our family faithfully trekked to this picture postcard town year after year. When the bell rang signaling the last day of school, I'd hop into our family's station wagon which would be jam-packed with groceries, toys, and clothes to last us until Labor Day rolled around. We spent three months in the great outdoors, inhaling the fresh air and enjoying nature's finest. We swam, we fished, and we hiked. It was during these times I felt unencumbered by the weight of my mother's sickness and instead filled many years with timeless memories.

Traverse City nestles up to Lake Michigan. Smaller lakes adorn the region. You can't drive five miles without seeing some body of water. Sometimes before we packed up our stuff and headed back to East Lansing for the first day of school, I would wake up to the sight of steam rising from the lake. The silky smooth surface of the water showed no movement, not even the slightest ripple, and reflected the trees embracing the shoreline. Even now as I write this, I can close my eyes and melt back into time with that image.

I can still smell the fresh pine scent of the wooden bunk beds in our cottage. I would lie there every night dreaming little girl dreams. My dreams weren't that original, but they were mine. I usually fantasized the garden-variety "Princess meets Prince Charming" but instead of spending forever in a giant castle with pink rooms and a moat protected by alligators, I spent happily-ever-after in Traverse City with my prince. I was obsessed with the princess storyline in my head. I remember waking up at 5 a.m. to watch Princess Diana marry Prince Charles. I was glued to the TV set and was blown away by her breathtaking gown and the royal extravaganza. I vowed to be like her when I grew up. Me and the rest of the nine-year-old girls out there.

When I graduated from high school, the dream of becoming a princess faded. I wanted to be a police officer, thanks to Jon and Ponch on *CHiPS*, but instead I attended Arizona State University. I was a poster child college kid and switched my major a few times.

Before I met my husband Mike in the summer before my sophomore year at college, I dated another guy for about a year. Like most giddy and naive girls, the first day I met this "man of my dreams," I swore he was absolutely perfect. Sweet. Kind. Loving. Caring. And hot. Super hot. I had won the college guy lottery, or so I thought.

One day I was sitting in class and struck up a conversation

with a new girl. We chatted about our favorite topic—our boyfriends. We swapped stories and realized our guys were very similar. Similar in tastes, similar in looks, similar in personalities. They even lived in the same dorm and on the same floor. The coincidences were alarming. They could only mean one thing. That's right, the little bugger was two-timing both of us. Oh, I forgot to mention he also gave us identical Christmas and Valentine's Day gifts. Not the most creative guy around.

It was the first time my heart was shattered. I was devastated beyond words. I spent the next several nights in my dorm, isolated from friends and ignoring social opportunities. I thought things like this only happened in the movies. It took me months before I even considered dating again, and even then, the thought made my stomach churn. I couldn't bear to be betrayed again and carefully constructed an emotional barricade.

I was back home in Michigan for summer break, just two weeks before I had to return to Arizona, when I met Mike at a bar. My parents weren't too happy, but what could they expect? I was in college. College kids congregate at bars, not in churches or at museums.

Thanks to my trusty fake ID (my parents don't know about that one), I was sipping on a white Zinfandel while hanging out with my girlfriends. It was a pretty classy drink for a spry chick like me, but beer made me sick. I got really drunk my first night of college and spent hours hugging the toilet and cutting my hair because it was hanging in my face and blocking my already shaky aim. I vowed never to drink beer again and haven't looked back since. Even now, the smell makes me want to run to the hills.

As I swished the rosy goodness in my equally as classy paper cup (don't you miss cheap college bars?), an adorable guy walked in wearing a baseball uniform. Beads of sweat trickled down his forehead and his matted hair stuck to the sides of his face. He was laughing with his buddies when out of nowhere our eyes met and he flashed me a million dollar grin. Oh, what a boy in a uniform could do to a small town girl like me.

We immediately clicked. Mike was six years older than me. Although I was only eighteen-years old, I felt like a grown-up talking to him. Knowing his age was like a prescription for instant maturation. I tried my best to put on a grown woman front and kept the fresh meat college girl at bay. I never told Mike how old I was. Somehow it was never brought up until the night before he proposed; only then did I divulge my little secret.

As the night crept into the early hours of the morning and the last of the drunk kids staggered out of the bar into the crisp air, I sat on a bar stool gazing into the dreamy eyes of a man with whom I had officially fallen into love...lust...like. Whatever it was, I was smitten. The more we spoke, the more I liked him. It was obvious Mike was going places. His confidence and enthusiasm for the possibilities and opportunities life had to offer were contagious. I wanted to know more about him. I wanted to know everything about him. Sigh. I just didn't want the night to end.

The timing, of course, couldn't have been worse. We had two dates that week and then I had to go back to school 3,000 miles away. We weren't going to let a small thing like geography stand in our way. Our long-distance relationship was romantic at first. We spent hours writing long letters, bathing each other in mushy compliments and trying to out-do each other in how much we missed the other. Our phone calls were equally full of schmaltz. But long-distance soon began to stink.

When Mike came to visit me in Arizona, I knew I had to

move back to Michigan. I didn't want distance to be a factor anymore. I was accepted at Western Michigan University, an hour and a half away from where Mike lived. It was the perfect situation. I was far enough away from him that I could still enjoy my college experience and spend time with my girl-friends, yet close enough so we could see each other regularly.

Sadly, timing wasn't on our side. Before I made the big move, Mike's company relocated him to St. Louis, Missouri. The plan was for him to stay there for a few months and move on to Kansas City. Two years later, Mike was still in St. Louis and I was officially a pro at making the six-hour drive to visit him. I could practically do it blindfolded.

Mike proposed in my last semester of college. I graduated with a degree in parks and recreation management with communications as a minor, and immediately plunged into wedding-planning mode. After all, I had the degree for it. We set the date for January 11, 1992. I couldn't wait to marry Mike and start a new life together. He was fun and brought out the best in me.

I never once thought about how different marriage was going to be since we had never lived together. For that matter, we never even lived nearby each other. My parents didn't prepare me for what living with a spouse was like. My expec-tations basically came from chick flicks, TV shows, and my naïve imagination. I assumed our living situation would be the same as living with my college roommates—a lot of bumping into each other, occasional screaming matches about being in the bathroom too long, and battles about who should clean what. Oh, and since he was my husband, a lot of cuddling, late night romantic talks, and spending every moment together in newlywed bliss.

In zero to sixty, I went from sharing a studio with three girls and eating pizza every night to sharing a home with a man with whom I would spend the rest of my life. I didn't know we would need to resolve boundary issues, or talk about who was responsible for doing what, or communicate what was expected of the other. I didn't enter the marriage with rose-colored glasses; I went in with blinders. I also wasn't prepared for doing the bulk of the cleaning, cooking, shopping, and bill-paying. The romantic notions of spending weekends in bed feeding each other gourmet meals that would be cooked by our maid and brought up by our butler were kaput.

Don't get me wrong. I loved being married. I loved being committed to a man who was always sure of himself, knew he was going to be a great success, and believed in great things for our future. I loved that about Mike. But that first year was full of growing pains for both us.

When finally given the chance to get to know each other inside and out, the good, the bad, and the quirky, we discovered a few things. Mike and I are as opposite as they come. I'm introverted and sensitive. Mike is outspoken and outgoing. My idea of a perfect evening is to curl up on the couch in front of the fireplace and watch an old movie. Mike would rather us put on our dancing shoes and paint the town red.

Though we spent much of this first year adjusting to one another and learning how to be ourselves together, one thing was certain. We loved each other and were in this marriage for the long haul.

When we started building our first house just outside of St. Louis in the small town of O'Fallon, I felt like I was in a daze most of the time. I was only twenty-two years old. What did I know about home building? Nothing. Absolutely nothing. Right before we took on this major undertaking, we were warned that the stress involved can do some damage to a marriage. From differences of opinions on carpet, paint, and even seemingly small stuff like cabinet knobs, to budgets that slowly but surely grow larger every day, to dealing with consistently late or no-show contractors—building a house is difficult. But here is where Mike and I found common ground. We both knew what we wanted and made quick decisions. We didn't need to spend hours poring over floor plans, furniture ideas, or layout options.

During this time we also learned what hard workers we were. We both wanted a lot out of life—financial success and the home with a white picket fence, lots of kids, and a dog who would greet us and bring us our slippers and the paper. While Mike was sure of his career in financial planning, I wasn't sure what I wanted to do. I just knew I wanted to work. Having a job gave me a purpose and something to look forward to. During college, my parents didn't want me to work in order for me to focus on studying and getting good grades, so when I graduated I was ready to bust out into the working world.

I took an internship for the city of St. Charles. I made a whopping $1,500 the entire time I was there, but I didn't care. I was in the job market and in some way I was making a difference. Because we needed as much money as possible to support ourselves and build our house, I spent my evening hours working at Baskin Robbins scooping ice cream. I was so embarrassed that I had to get a second job, I never told my parents. To this day, they don't know I worked at the famous 31-flavors chain. With Mike getting home from work every day close to 10 p.m. and me getting home a half hour after that, you can imagine how exhausted we were. I won't lie. Not seeing each other enough put a strain on our marriage.

When I found out I was pregnant, I was so excited. Sara was born on December 1, 1993. She loved the womb so much, she refused to come out for a few weeks and when she did, she surprised us at 9 pounds, 10 ounces. That's a big baby! She was breathing much too fast and it worried the doctors. In the delivery room, my baby was whisked away from me, amidst the clamor of hurried footsteps and concerned whispers of the staff. Sara was rushed to the intensive care unit; I didn't see her for 24 hours.

We made it home healthy and happy after a few days; I had to adjust to being a new mom. Getting used to living with my husband was one thing. Getting used to a newborn was something totally different. Mike wasn't dependent on me to feed, clean, hold, or soothe him; nor did he expect me to figure out what he wanted whenever he'd bawl his eyes out. Dealing with a new baby pushed me into this unusual space where I had to deal with a new kind of change that came with many conflicting feelings.

My days felt manic. One day I was tired from getting by on only four hours of sleep; the next I was flying high hearing my little girl make cute burps and gurgles. One day I was stressed and ready to pull out every single hair in my head; and the next I was enveloped in bliss holding a calm and sleeping baby. I was like any other new mom, caring for a totally dependent newborn. No book, teacher, or even parent could prepare me for this. But I realized something within the first few days of caring for Sara; I loved motherhood. That's why I had five kids.

Two years later on February 7, 1996, we welcomed Taylor into this world. All my children were born with a penchant for drama. Taylor had what doctors thought was a seizure and was taken to a nearby children's hospital right after he was born. But like his strong older sister, he was fine after a few days. Taylor was my happy baby. He was content in all circumstances. He was a mother's dream.

Baby number three was a shocker. After seeing the plus sign on the pregnancy test, the infamous blue symbol that had elated me twice before, I was in disbelief. Three more tests and sixty bucks less in my wallet, I knew I had to own up to the truth—I was having a baby. Unfortunately, the timing wasn't the best. Our financial situation did not factor in another baby. It barely factored in the four of us.

I called my parents to tell them the news. After I spent the first few minutes of the call heaving with sobs and blowing my runny nose, my mother blurted out, "Can you afford it?" Of course we couldn't. Mike had just graduated from the University of Missouri at St. Louis and had given up his safe salary to start out in the insurance business. He traded working for a company that had paid him a chunky salary for one that offered the best in training but a low, commission-based paycheck.

My dad was instrumental in calming me down and saying the six words that we all need to hear once in a while, "Everything is going to be fine." And it was, except Brendan came a few weeks early on January 13, 1998 (drama, drama, drama!). The little daredevil that he was and still is, he wanted out of the womb as soon as possible.

With a houseful of children, I became the master at teaching my kids the art of waiting and being patient. You can't feed and hold them all at once. Our house was chaotic with a four-year-old, a two-year old, and a newborn. Nobody, including me, was getting sleep. Everyone, including me, was crying. Mike was working most of the day struggling to provide for us with the little he was earning.

I had a rough time and it showed. We lived in a neighborhood where the mothers seemed to have it all together all the time. They made raising a family seem as easy as microwaving a TV dinner. They walked down the block with their blown out coifs and sparkling smiles, parading their little munchkins around in matching clothes and sporting top-of-the-line baby gear. And there I was, pulling teeth just to find some clean clothes that my kids and I could wear as I tried hard not to qualify as the top candidate for the Impatient-Annoyed-Frustrated-and-Tired Mother of the Year award.

While I spent a few years wrapped up in dirty diapers, baby food and spit up, Mike always had his nose in a Tony Robbins book or was listening to self-help tapes in the car, the office, or at home. Back then, I didn't understand what he was doing or how it was an investment of his time for our future because I was immersed in a world of babies. But that diligence in focusing on his personal self-growth is ultimately what helped catapult him into bigger and better things.

I admire Mike for his dedication and persistence. He always had a desire and an unwavering confidence that he was going to be successful. Honestly, I didn't share that resolution most of time, but his conviction was so strong I believed in him with my whole heart and did whatever I could to help him reach his goals. From the first day we met, Mike was always writing down his goals or inspirational reminders. It wasn't uncommon for me to stumble into our bathroom early in the morning and wash my face in front of a mirror covered with yellow Post-it notes with quotes from Norman Vincent Peale, Abraham Lincoln, or Napoleon Hill.

Even though the pay was crummy, my husband believed working for Northwestern Mutual Life would provide him a future worth having. While this move paid off down the road and we are now reaping the benefits of his hard work, getting there was a ruthless climb, kind of like wearing Jimmy Choo stilettos up Mount Fuji. One month, our finances were in order; the next month, we couldn't afford groceries. The instability and inconsistency made me nuts because we had three kids to raise. If it had been just me, fine; I would have had three jobs and lived on SPAM, but I couldn't be that flexible with three kids counting on my energy, time, and money.

When Mike came home from work, I didn't greet him with a hug and a kiss every day. Most times, I pestered him with questions. "Did you make any money today?" "Did you make a sale?" "What did you do all day?" My poor husband. I tried my best not to be a nag, but I couldn't help it. While he was at work, I was at home fielding calls from bill collectors and trying to figure out if we had enough money to pay for the electricity. It wasn't fun and I wanted to make sure he wasn't spending his days playing golf or sipping cognac with some head honchos. Looking back, my level of distrust was horrendous, but I've learned a lot since those days.

Although I loved motherhood, having three kids under the age of four and having only a couple of bucks trickling in here and there gave my already anxious tendencies an unwanted boost. We were falling behind in our bills and I felt overwhelmed. I never wanted to admit it, but I needed help; I couldn't do this by myself anymore. All I wanted was to move to a place where I felt safe and at peace. A place I could comfortably call home. I realized I wanted to move to Traverse City, my summer childhood refuge.

Hoping a fresh change would help both of us and relieve the mounting pressure we felt, we moved to my paradise in the fall of 1998. I couldn't have been more thrilled. I packed up our three babies, two cats, and our dog and we came home. I couldn't wait to share a taste of my childhood with my own children. When we settled down, my parents also moved from East Lansing to Traverse City. We were one big happy family.

Things started to look up. Mike was making more money and I was pitching in with his business and even started selling Mary Kay products on the side. As soon as I lost most of the weight I had gained from my three pregnancies, I found out I was pregnant again. Morgan, our fourth addition, was born on March 12, 2001, without any complications. She was a happy, healthy baby and thankfully had an uneventful delivery.

❦

Two years later, Mike decided it was time to move on from Northwestern Mutual and work independently. As a financial planner, he wanted to offer a wider variety of products to his clients. I believe financial planning is his true calling. Mike has a heart for people and wanted to help them by showing how they could protect their assets. He rented a small office not too far from home and started working out of that building in July of 2003.

When Mike outgrew his office, he had to hire a staff person to help with the administrative details. We couldn't afford it, so I agreed to work nights at a local grocery store stocking shelves. I worked there during the holiday season, but quickly realized it would be an impossible gig to maintain. I was tired, getting no sleep, and was sick all the time. Caring for the kids all day and working at night made me a grouch (and that's being kind). For the well-being and sanity of our family and me, I knew I couldn't do it. We opted to cut our budget instead and save every penny we could.

That spring I found out I was pregnant again. Mike and I ran the gamut of emotions—from excitement to bewilderment to shock. I hadn't yet shared the news with anyone besides my husband. Just before I headed out the door for my second visit with my obstetrician, Sara came running behind me and proudly patted my belly. "You're pregnant, Mommy," she beamed. How did she know? I have no idea but her affirmation soothed me.

The doctor's visit, unfortunately, wasn't so comforting. As I lay on the cold, cushioned table wearing the flimsy cloth gown that every woman jokes about and hates, I closed my eyes and tried to relax. My doctor and I engaged in small talk for a while and he made a well-meaning joke about me being fertile. As he moved forward with the examination, his demeanor and the atmosphere in the room changed. I was far enough along in my pregnancy that he should have been able to detect the baby's heartbeat with a stethoscope. After about a minute of having him maneuver the shiny round object all over my abdomen, I knew something was wrong. There was no heartbeat.

The doctor ordered an ultrasound. I couldn't make out anything on the monitor, but it was obvious nothing was moving. The baby had died, he gently informed me, and I had to wait for my body to naturally miscarry the fetus. I was a wreck. A beautiful gift had been ripped out of my hands. And now I had to wait for it to come out of my body? I didn't know what that entailed or what to expect. Even thinking about it makes me cringe.

I stumbled out of the doctor's office, numb from shock, and hardly paid attention to the nurse's kind words of consolation. I drove straight to my parent's house sobbing the entire way. I was heartbroken. They tried their best to comfort me but they couldn't take the pain away. No one could. Nothing could. It was something I simply had to deal with.

I miscarried a week and a half later. I wasn't prepared for the incredible amount of blood and the pain. It felt like I was giving birth. From the time the cramping began in the evening until the sun rose the next day, I just lay on the bathroom floor with my head on the cool tile floor. I stayed locked in that tiny room until it was all over. Until the sight of blood was no longer visible. Until the last wave of cramps left my body. Until all signs of the baby I had once carried had disappeared.

I was a zombie for a while, but with four other kids at home, I had to snap out of it pretty fast. There is no explaining "miscarriage" to children. I couldn't give excuses for not cooking and cleaning, or for sleeping so much because my baby died. I had to go on, business as usual. "Pull up your bootstraps and suck it up," was my motto. And that's just what I did.

Two years later, on September 15, 2005, I was blessed with my daughter Madison. One of the most wonderful parts of the delivery was that her big sister Sara got to be there to witness her birth. Sara was thirteen at the time. Not only did she witness the birth, she was also the first to give Madison a bath and dress her.

About four years after our last child was born, our family went from being broke to Mike owning two successful companies. His predictions were accurate. My husband was finally on top of the game and reaping the rewards of the hard work he had sown since he was in his early twenties. On many levels, our lives were totally different. But it wasn't just about the money. Yes, we weren't struggling any more. Yes, we could afford to take luxurious vacations. Yes, we were able to buy expensive cars. But I found more awaited me than material objects I never thought I'd be able to attain.

I discovered that whoever said, "The only problems that money can solve are money problems" was right. I learned the hard way that money can't buy you peace. Money can't buy you a healthy lifestyle. Money can't buy you friends. Money can't buy you security. Oh sure, money can probably buy you a faux version of those things, but just like an imitation Louis you can get on the sidewalks of NYC's Canal Street, it's not going to last. I was the wife of a millionaire and I found myself lonely, lost, and burned out. And it took a tragedy for me to start asking some questions I wasn't completely ready to answer.

3
Loss

"When you are sorrowful look again in your heart, and you shall see that in truth you are weeping for that which has been your delight."
~ Kahlil Gibran

The phone couldn't have rung at a worse time. Holding the vacuum cleaner in one hand, writing down more tasks to my already mile-long to-do list with my other hand, and using my biggest outside voice to ask my husband if he had picked up Sara's birthday cake, I groaned. I almost dropped everything at the sound of the ear-splitting ring. It was annoying. Loud. And inopportune.

I was cleaning up, preparing the house on a chilly November day in 2007. In only a few days our home would be filled with ten teenage girls celebrating my oldest daughter's birthday. In only a few days, the house would echo with high-pitched giggles and breathless commentaries splattered with words and phrases like "no way," "whatever," and "like," about how cute a certain boy is, or the best place to shop in the mall, or how mean teacher such-and-such is. The house that I was painstakingly cleaning to showcase what a neat and orderly mom I was (move out, June Cleaver, move in Becky Reese) was soon going to be trashed with hair products, clothes, and makeup. And, of course, there would be the mountains of Doritos and other snacks only teenage girls can eat in monstrous portions because of their supersonic metabolism. But in reality, the stress of those things was nothing compared to what I would find out on the other end of the ringing phone.

I dropped the vacuum cleaner with an alarming thud, praying I didn't scratch the hardwood floor, and picked up the phone. "Hello," I blurted out without even trying to mask my irritation.

"Becky?" My brother Andy was on the other line. "I, I'm calling because…because…it's about Carol." I wondered why he was stuttering so much. It sounded like he was getting choked up. Maybe this was a practical joke?

"Andy, I can't understand you. What did you say about our sister?"

"I'm so sorry, Beck. The police found her body this morning. Becky, she's dead." When Andy's voice cracked in the two-syllable sound of my name, I knew he wasn't kidding. My heart dropped to the floor and my hands began to shake. I was trying to process the life-changing words of my sister being dead, but the noise and chaos of my five kids scurrying around the kitchen was overwhelming.

"Quiet," I yelled while holding the phone away from my mouth. "Stop! Go upstairs! Now!!" I hesitantly positioned the phone back to my ear, but I would much rather have hung it up. I didn't want to know more. I didn't want to hear more. I didn't want any more news that would confirm that my sister was, in fact, dead. I wanted to pretend it wasn't true, that it was a joke or a misunderstanding, or that maybe my brother got his facts wrong. After Andy gave me more information that I couldn't fully digest in the hazy blur of shock, we said our goodbyes.

My sister is dead. I thought of my parents, whom my brother had tried to call right before me. I knew they were on their way home from church. I knew as my Mom made lunch, my dad would be checking the messages on the answering machine. In the midst of tossing salad and slapping together sandwiches, they would hear the news that their oldest daughter was dead. They would have to bury their own child. There was no way they could handle such horrible news in such a cold and impersonal way.

I had to get over there and fast. My body quivered and my eyes glazed over as I stared at the telephone that was so innocently cradled in the phone charger, oblivious to the crushing blow it had delivered only seconds ago. "I have to go to my parents," I repeated over and over to no one in particular. My voice echoed in the empty kitchen. I knew what I had to do, but I just couldn't move. My feet were firmly planted to the floor as if stuck in a block of concrete. "I have to go to my parent's house," I said again, this time just as Mike rounded the corner.

I looked at my husband blankly. "Carol's dead. I've got to tell my parents before they hear it on the machine." Mike looked horrified and held me for a few minutes. I couldn't hear or feel a thing. Not his warm whispers of comfort. Not his arms wrapped around me. Not him holding my hand and leading me to the car that he said he would drive to his in-laws. The present moment was spinning in a whirlwind without logic or sense and all I could manage was to numbly walk through it, step by step.

Mike and I rode in silence as I stared out the window, the familiar fifteen-minute drive nothing but a blurry mesh of houses, buildings, and trees. My parents, as always, were delighted to see me, but they balked when I told them to sit down, that I had some bad news for them. If it weren't for the shock shrouding my body and my mind, I would not have been able to relay the message. My hypnotic state temporarily pushed aside my emotions and gave me the courage to say, "Andy just called. Carol's dead."

My dad refused to sit down and kept walking around in circles, his eyes brimming with tears that unhurriedly cascaded down his wrinkled cheeks. My mom screamed. Her wailing soon changed to a barrage of questions. "How? When?" She wanted to know details but I had only the bits and pieces my brother told me. "I don't know, Mom. Andy just said she didn't show up at work and they sent the police over to the house. They found her body."

Still pacing around the kitchen, my father kept saying odd things like, "It was bound to happen one day." He started to hook the dog up to the leash to take her for a walk and softly whispered that no parents should have to bury their own child. Then he sighed and said something about how he imagined it was time. With eight healthy kids and relatively few problems in the family, my dad felt like a lucky man. It wasn't that he was waiting for the shoe to drop, but I guess he knew tragedy of some kind was inevitable. As a parent, he had evaded this kind of suffering for a long time. I knew he was in shock; I was, too.

The coroner wanted someone to identify the body and my parents didn't have the heart to do it. It would be my job. When my dad was able to pull himself together, the three of us sat at the table, called the travel agent, and booked me a flight to San Diego. I was scheduled to fly out in a few hours. I left my grieving parents with warm hugs. They needed to call the rest of the family and inform them of the news.

There wasn't much else to say or do. In times of inexplicable tragedy, words are pointless. And though we shared the same loss, the sorrow that my dad, my mom, and I were going through was unique and personal. We were experiencing different dialects of the same sad language.

I took two-year-old Madison with me to California. On the three-hour flight I thought of the recent trip Madison, Morgan, my mom, and I had taken to visit Carol. We had spent a day at Disneyland. The girls had so much fun riding the shuttles back and forth from the parking lot to the entrance that we delayed going into the park. They were so young, they thought it was an actual ride and loved it. But once they set foot in downtown Disney, they went bonkers salivating at the princess dresses and squealing over the countless Disney characters that lavished them with attention.

My sister and I spent much time together on that trip, especially because Madison was colicky and the only way she could be soothed to sleep was by driving her around. Carol and I talked for hours every night while Madison got her rest. I'm so thankful I was able to spend that time with my big sister.

Life is fleeting. We all know it deep down in our hearts, but it usually takes us being sucker-punched by a tragedy to truly appreciate that truth. Not only did my sister's death make me grateful for the close relationship we shared, it also created in me a deep hole I was unable to fill. With her gone, I noticed how much I had depended on and needed her. Through her death, I came face to face with the troubling fact that I was lost. I had been lost for quite some time, but with my sister in my life I was able to camouflage my off-course identity through her comforting friendship and the fun things we did together.

The truth was that over the last several years, I had immersed myself in motherhood and supporting my husband as he bettered himself in his personal and professional development. Like most women, I fell into the trap of putting everybody and everything before me... all the time. I got caught up in the strangulating grip of a fast-paced life. I became a victim to always being available through cell phones, email, and texts and consequently mismanaged my boundaries. In this tangled spider web, I lost my identity, I lost my sense of self, and I lost my independence. Perhaps more importantly, I realized that in losing myself, I had lost my purpose.

At the time, having Carol around seemed therapeutic because it allowed me to ignore those dark feelings. When I talked to her, I felt good about myself because I could share my true heart and she always made me feel better, either by her words or by whisking me off to some fancy spa for a massage, to a couture boutique where we'd do some retail damage, or to a world famous restaurant where the portions were tiny but the bill was astronomical. When she was gone, I had to face myself and finally admit that I was in need of some serious changes. Ugh. I didn't like that place at all. I just wanted my sister back.

Though she was sixteen years older than me, Carol was my best friend. We were polar opposites in many ways. She was outgoing; I'm quiet. She loved the fast paced life; I prefer a slower speed. She was glitzy and glamorous; I had everything to learn about style. Regardless of our differences, we were bonded by more than blood, we were bonded by friendship. True friendship.

While we had not gotten to know each other very well until Sara was born in 1993, I always looked up to my big sister. We stayed in touch over the years, but when I finished college and became a newlywed, I didn't have a lot of extra time to stay connected to Carol. She, however, never failed to reach out. She'd always send me thoughtful cards and leave me caring messages about how she was thinking of me.

Carol was the quintessential big sister. As a kid, I would raid her closet and spend hours in her bedroom playing dress-up. I was fascinated by her million tubes of bright lipstick, wands of mascara, and blush brushes. When she came home from college, I remember curling up on her bed right on top of her fur coat, drifting off to sleep as I breathed in its sweet scent and cuddled on the inviting fur. I loved the silky feel of the luxurious lining and running my fingers through the supple mink fur. Wrapping the coat around me, I pretended I was a princess taking a beauty nap on a bear rug.

My sister spent a few years at Michigan Tech, where she was the college beauty queen, and then landed a fabulous gig as a professional shopper and food critic. She worked for a company that reviewed high-end hotels, restaurants, and casinos. Carol flew all over the country, stopping in chic places like Las Vegas and New York. There she indulged in a luxurious lifestyle at her company's expense while evaluating every aspect of how the establishment she was visiting was run. I was lucky. Carol was kind enough to snag me away for a few days here and there to tag along on her glamorous trips.

My big sister was my well-versed tour guide into the world of glitz and glamour. Because of her profession, she gave me crash courses in expensive makeup, spa treatments, and high-end fashion and introduced me to luxury hotels and five star restaurants. We met several times in Las Vegas. I remember getting my first facial with her at the MGM Hotel. I felt silly because I had never had a facial and didn't know what to expect. I didn't understand how these beauticians were going to cleanse and moisturize my face any differently than the way I had been doing it for the last twenty years of my life. Boy, was I in for a big surprise.

When Mike and I were struggling with our bills, going to visit my sister in some exotic hotel, resort, or spa was a welcome break. We laughed and chatted the weekend away eating the best foods and staying in places I couldn't possibly afford. We drank $150 bottles of champagne. While the bubbly extravagance warmly made its way down my throat, all I could think about was how I was practically swallowing a week's worth of grocery money. We feasted on $100 Kobe steaks, desserts flown in from Paris, and international delicacies that were hard to pronounce but tasted like heaven.

The glitz and glamour was part of her job, but to me it was a world of its own. A world unlike anything I had ever known. A world I didn't even know existed. Between my sister and the great pleasures of couture shopping, room service and fine dining, I forgot about my troubles. My world in Michigan was far behind me. I felt like I was living in a fairy tale, not living in my real world of feeling disconnected from myself and discontent with my life.

In December following the 9/11 terrorist attacks, Sara and I met Carol in New York City. She was rating a fabulous hotel and thought it would be fun to plan a girl's trip. What I remember most is having the sobering opportunity to witness the aftermath of the attacks. We walked through downtown and paused at the countless number of posters that lined the sidewalks and featured pictures of men and women, young and old, of different ages and ethnicities who had died on that fateful day.

We saw snapshots of police officers, fire fighters, employees who worked in and around the World Trade Center, and people who just happened to be passing by the wrong place at the wrong time. They were all missing and their photos were posted by loved ones who desperately hoped they were still alive somewhere in the unrecognizable dust and rubble of tall buildings, stores, and subways. The three of us held hands and no one dared utter a word as we walked. We felt heaviness at the loss as we wiped tears away from our eyes. Even Sara, at the tender age of nine, noticed the burdened feeling. I believe the walk knit Carol and me even closer.

That night we went to dinner and joked about what kind of man Sara was going to marry. Sara, bold and hardheaded even as a child, had already decided what her husband would be and look like, how many kids they would have and what their names were going to be and, of course, where they were going to live. Over a delicious five-course meal, my sister took copious notes of the life Sara was confident she was destined to have. As we savored bite after bite of mouthwatering chocolate trifle, Carol told us she planned on reading this list at Sara's wedding to see how much of it came true. She would never get the chance. I spent a few heartbreaking hours searching my sister's home for this piece of paper, but I have yet to come across it. I truly believe God will help me find it one day.

Madison and I were en route to California. As I listened to the captain's announcement that we would be landing in twenty minutes, the good memories came to a screeching halt. I started thinking about my sister's death and the fact that she was no longer a physical part of my life. How would her absence affect me? I was used to talking to her on the phone every day if not two or three times a day. It was a habit I didn't break until her death. Carol gave me the space and grace to talk freely, fully expressing my thoughts and opinions, no matter how crazy, irrational, or strange she might have thought they were. She listened to me. She gave sound advice when she could. And she never judged. I would miss our talks the most.

I knew Carol hadn't been feeling well. She had gained an extraordinary amount of weight. No one knew why. She never talked about it and we never pressed the issue. When I saw her last in September before she died, she looked exhausted. I could see how the extra weight was physically limiting her. My sister could barely climb up the stairs and got out of breath doing the simplest things. I expressed my concern and she nodded like a robot saying, "I know, Beck, I know. I've got to find a new doctor to help me."

On that trip, Carol gave me a bunch of jewelry. When she spread the mass of diamond bracelets, elegant gemstone neck-laces, and sparkling earrings over her bed, she seemed elated to let me have so much of her beautiful stuff. She always gave from the depths of her heart; it was something I always appre-ciated about my sister.

When Madison and I arrived at Carol's apartment after sunset, my brother Chris was waiting for me. I walked into her home and felt chills tingle up and down my spine. Her apart-ment was beautifully furnished with classic artwork and delicate antique vases. Pale pink colors and fresh flowers illu-minated the otherwise dark apartment and showcased her elegant style.

Everything in my sister's house represented an owner who was still alive. There were a few dirty dishes in the sink. There was some money and a bank deposit slip on the kitchen table. And not only was her computer on, but so was her Instant Messenger. Carol had been chatting online with our brother Andy right before she had the heart attack.

The police and firemen who arrived at the scene were respectful of Carol's belongings and didn't mess up the apart-ment. They had only removed her driver's license out of her wallet so they could identify the body and carefully laid it back on top of the wallet on the table. Nothing else had been touched. Nothing was out of place. I expected at any moment to see Carol burst through the door and give me a hug, excited about my surprise visit. "Joke's on you," she would tell me with a beaming smile. "You're on Candid Camera."

But there was—and there would be—no Carol. While Chris and I no longer had to confirm her identity, we had to take care of the funeral arrangements while she was prepared for the autopsy. When I saw my sister's lifeless body in the coffin for the first time, I went numb. I didn't believe she was gone even though I was eye-to-eye with her flesh, a mere casing of her spirit, her temporary home.

I had to touch her. I just had to. I had to know she was really gone. I stretched my hand out over her arm and gently pressed down. I jumped back as soon as I felt her cold, hard, and waxy skin. I couldn't hide in denial anymore. My sister was dead. Her life was over. My best friend was gone.

The funeral was surreal. Everything was a blur, but I vividly remember Madison running around the funeral parlor. It was the first time I noticed how light her hair was, much lighter than Mike's or mine. It was almost blonde. Just then it hit me. Madison was a spitting image of Carol. She was my sister living on in spirit, living on in life. One of the songs they played at the funeral was "Somewhere over the Rainbow." Anytime I hear it now, it makes me stop in my tracks. How appropriate is that song for her life? Carol taught me to search for my pot of gold at the end of the rainbow.

Sometimes repercussions of a tragedy are triggered and felt years later. Recently, Sara got into a bad car wreck and totaled her car. She slid on black ice and smashed head-on into a tree. The collision was so powerful, the tree split in half. Luckily Sara walked out of the totaled vehicle with just a sprained arm and lots of bruises.

When I got the call, Morgan suddenly became sick and

told me she was going to bed. She later told me she heard part of the conversation where the police and ambulance were on their way. Imagining the accident scene and her fear of not knowing whether or not her sister was okay reminded Morgan of Aunt Carol's death. She didn't know how to handle it other than to hide out for a while.

Though Morgan was only six at the time, she remembers the feeling of overwhelming sadness in the pit of her stomach. I could feel my daughter's pain and was overcome with emotion at how much my sister meant to my little girl. Morgan's flashback also brought to mind how Sara developed epileptic type symptoms when my sister passed away. For years afterward, any time she got stressed out or upset, she would shake uncontrollably. Doctors finally connected the dots and told us it had to do with the trauma Sara went through with her aunt's death. She meant a lot to them, more than she probably ever knew. My son Brendan has also told me how sometimes when he hears the phone ring or whenever I go into panic-mode, he relives the pain of losing Aunt Carol. I'm sure my sister would be touched by how profoundly her passing impacted my children.

Carol's death left me to question who I was. It put me on the track to seeking more out of myself, more out of life, more out of the mere existence I had been living for so long. I knew I had to get myself out of the rut I was in. I had to confront my fears and brush them aside. I had to step out of the comfort zone I was in. I had to stop paying attention to what others thought or said about me.

Finding myself had nothing to do with fancy clothes, car, homes, or luxurious vacation spots. The transformation came from working through my inner fears. In fact, one of my motivators was the realization that Mike did not fall in love with the "lost" me. I was an independent, strong, and intelligent woman when we were first married. But somehow during my marriage and especially in our new life of having more money, I lost the independent and strong part. If Mike fell in love with someone I wasn't anymore, what does that mean? It was a scary question to ask myself, and one of many to come, but it was the start of a sometimes painful journey I had to take.

We don't lose ourselves overnight. I certainly didn't. It took a long period of time and a mesh of happenings that led to my internal disconnect. Trying to play an Oscar-worthy role as Super Mom and Super Wife probably contributed to my identity crisis. When Mike chose the path of starting his own business, I did whatever I could do to help him succeed. What loving spouse wouldn't? I did what I could because I loved him and I wanted the best for him.

I didn't nag him about how long he worked at the office; most nights he didn't come home until eight at night and, of course, he left early in the morning. I didn't complain when he spent every extra dime we had on self-development books, tapes, workshops, and out-of-town conferences. I didn't complain when I was in charge of putting together his mailings for work, like the three to five thousand invitations I would have to print, fold, stuff, address, stamp, and mail out once a month. When our kids got older, I enlisted their help. It once took a team of us eight hours to get the task done.

Mike's business skyrocketed, even after he split with his partner and we had to deal with some long-winded and costly legal battles. He always made evident his confidence that he would be a success. And guess what? He was right. Our bank accounts started getting bigger. We started traveling more, could afford nicer things, and I didn't need to be creative in figuring out where we were going to get the money to pay what bill first. I should have been happy, but I wasn't. I was miserable. I was stuck between two realms—feeling lost in the shuffle and knowing, in the deepest part of my heart, that there was more for me out there. Problem was, I didn't know exactly what that 'more' was or how to get there.

I invested myself in my children. Not that it's a bad thing. Every mother needs to be whole-heartedly dedicated to her family. It's a crucial ingredient in raising healthy kids. But as a Super Mom of five kids, I couldn't see that being a good woman, mother and wife meant taking some time for myself— whether it was to exercise, read a book, take a half hour bubble bath, whatever. I just thought my life purpose was to feed all of my hopes, energy, purpose, and time into my children.

But doing that not only made me feel drained and wiped out, it also contributed to my weight gain. Granted, I was pumping out baby after baby and if you're a mom, you know how difficult it is to take off baby weight, especially if you find yourself pregnant all the time.

And another thing. It's pretty easy to cover up weight gain in Michigan. It's cold most of the time, so you always have to bundle up. With five kids, frigid weather, and continual snow falling five months out of the year, I learned how to live in sweatpants and sweatshirts. I started neglecting my appear- ance, even after I could afford all the flattering and expensive clothes I wanted. I was comfortable in my sweats. They were a haven. I could hide in them and be safe from the outside world. But hiding only buried my true self even deeper.

From spending most of my entire young and adult life trying to please people, I had assumed my martyrdom behavior would in turn provide me with a quiet and calm happy place in my soul. Not true. There was no happy place, just a floundering sense of self. Even though I was in a financially happy place after my sister's death, I was still plagued by anxiety of the world I was used to. Even though I was no longer struggling to pay my bills or needing to worry about lawsuits, payroll, or paying our mortgage bill, I was still stuck in "what if" mode.

What if it things fell apart? What if Mike's business took a nosedive and we lost everything? What if the kids got really sick? What if we get sued again? I had no sense of peace and my feeling of being lost grew bigger and bigger each day.

But money wasn't my biggest worry. Since Carol had died, I felt alone for the first time in my life. Alone and having to battle with questions that I had not had to face of where the real me had gone and who the real me is. I wish I could say my sister's death immediately catapulted me into taking better care of myself, but it didn't. What it did was turn the page to a new chapter in my life of finally realizing I had to take care of myself. But I didn't know how. I didn't know where to start. And sadly, I had no one to talk to about it.

4
Finding Friends in all the Wrong Places

"The best time to make friends is before you need them."
~ Ethel Barrymore

⸻

I'll never forget reading an article about loneliness that referenced authors John Cacioppo and William Patrick's book *Loneliness: Human Nature and the Need for Social Connection.* These authors say that about 20% or about 60 million people in this country feel lonely. Duke University researchers found that between 1985 and 2004, the number of people who said they had no one with whom to talk about important matters tripled. When I read these statistics, I was shocked. I didn't realize so many people, including me, were lonely. Ironically, the information made me feel less lonely.

For much of my adult life, I battled loneliness. Saying I was lonely was embarrassing to admit. The first time I said it out loud, I broke down and cried. I felt ashamed even though no one besides me heard my confession. When Carol died, the emptiness surfaced. Though I had a best friend (I use that term loosely) in town, the friendship was one-sided. It was nothing like what I had with my sister.

Whereas this one friend spent most of our time talking

about herself, and only here and there was I able to interject some comments to help her with her problems, Carol and I rode down the two-lane highway of friendship. So when my big sister was gone, I was put in a position to evaluate my current friendship with this woman. Admitting the truth broke my heart.

When I first moved to Traverse City, it was hard to fit in. Deep down inside, I wanted to belong to a girl's club, you know have a handful of friends who hung out all the time, knew everything about each other and their families, and was always dropping by the house for coffee or a glass or two of wine. Kind of like what you see on the Real Housewives of This-or-That-Town. I had felt the same kind of yearning in high school. All I saw around me were cliques of girls who stuck together like Velcro, like sisters. I wanted an in with a clique, any clique, but instead found myself collecting a random friend here and there. Never a close-knit circle. When I got older, I felt that same need to belong, but it was even harder to find.

When you have to take care of five children, it's difficult to invest in friendships. That's why I felt lucky to have my sister around. And that's why when she died, I was crushed and felt more abandoned than ever. Maybe I was asking for too much. I didn't want the kind of girl squad that looked like the ones I saw on TV; I wanted healthy relationships, not gossip trains or superficial connections.

My idea of having a great circle of girlfriends is not sitting around a marble island in some lady's kitchen sipping on wine and viciously talking about whoever is not present at that moment. I'm sure you know the kind of women I'm talking about. The kind who are sickeningly sweet to you and call you pet names like "love" and "sugar," but behind your back tell your friends how cheap, selfish, fat, or misguided you are. And all that with saccharine smiles pasted on their faces.

I also wanted to steer clear of energy-suckers. The kind of people who use you in some way to build themselves up. They criticize you and make you feel bad about yourself. They call themselves your friends but when you need them the most, they are mysteriously never around. Oh yeah, and they talk about themselves or their problems constantly, without giving even a passing thought to how you are feeling or doing.

Perhaps I seem a bit jaded. Well, maybe, but I've not had the best of luck in this area of my life. I've had my share of superficial friendships and I've had my share of energy suckers. I'm not nearly as jaded as I used to be. Not by a long shot. And I'm well aware that my broken relationships were not entirely the fault of the other parties. I'm not proud to admit it, but I've got traits in me that just might have led to an unhealthy relationship or two. I'm learning how to better master the art of having friends without being an enabler, a problem-solver, or the golden ticket to someone's internal and external happiness.

Sometimes we are lucky to have friends for life. Other times, we are left with broken relationships that however painful teach us the power of forgiveness, help us find strength in our weakness, and show us where our trust and dependence lie. This was the experience I had with a woman named Stacey.

When I first met her in 2004, I was convinced she came into my life to offer the kind of relationship I had with my sister. I was sadly mistaken. The two had met several times and Stacey seemed jealous or perhaps intimidated by how close Carol and I were. I knew it was because Stacey didn't have much of a relationship with her own family.

Though our friendship ended on a bitter note, I learned a lot about the importance of genuine friendships. I trusted this woman with my thoughts, my insecurities, my husband's business, even my money. When my relationship with Stacey dissolved, it left a lot of anger and resentment on both our parts in its wake. And the loneliness I had originally felt from my sister's death multiplied.

I'll never forget the day I met her. I walked into my husband's office and was greeted by a petite blonde bombshell with boob spillage that was impossible to ignore. She was like a high school cheerleader packaged with the perfect body, bubbly personality, and oozing sexual charm. While she was friendly, I wasn't thrilled with her working for Mike. It wasn't just because she was smoking hot, but because Mike hired her from a guy who had an office down the hall from us. This particular man had a bad reputation around town for conducting unethical activities, and I didn't want anyone near Mike who could possibly be guided by an unscrupulous compass.

I was curious to see if she was worth the money she was being paid, money I knew Mike couldn't afford. He needed help around the office but our budget at the time wasn't very cushy. Stacey quickly dived into her marketing responsibilities and surprised me. She did a great job.

After a few months, my initial judgments tempered until they finally went away. Stacey and I started spending more time together and I started to like her. She was sweet and funny and I enjoyed hanging out with her. Before I knew it, we became running buddies. Every morning we'd meet at the house and plan our daily runs. We'd run three, five, seven miles around the scenic shores of our town and through evergreen tree-lined trails.

Stacey even talked me into doing my first half marathon when I was six months pregnant with Madison. As we ran toward the finish line, she joked about pretending to be my security guard to make sure everyone got out of the way of the wide pregnant woman coming through.

In October of 2006, we ran our first marathon together in Detroit. Warming up at the starting line, we were awestruck by the hundreds of runners shoulder to shoulder beside us gearing up for the 26.2-mile race. (Did you know that's 44,500 steps?) Some stretched. Some jogged in place. Some looked focused. Some were laughing. I'm sure most of us were a little nervous, trying to soothe the butterflies that were fluttering around our bellies.

Mile after mile Stacey and I trudged through the race, energized by the screaming crowds, getting much-welcomed water and bananas at the break stations, and encouraging the other when one was tired. Well, truth was, Stacey did a great job encouraging me. It was a challenging race and she helped bolster my confidence with positive affirmations and even ran to the store to get me some Tylenol because I was in so much pain. When we staggered to the finish line, we practically fell into each other's arms in amazement. It was an incredible feat to accomplish and even more rewarding when sharing it with a best friend. I felt the race bonded Stacey and me for life.

During this time, Stacey was working with Mike on a separate company, an online format of his regular business that seemed to be draining the bank account. Though money was steadily coming into the business, it never stayed put. It seemed whatever cash came in was quickly funneled through this account and then vanished. I remember briefly looking over the numbers and feeling a gnawing in my gut that something wasn't right. But I didn't pay attention. I simply shooed away any feeling that might imply Stacey wasn't making a full effort to make the business profitable.

I didn't even want to know if anything weird was going on because for the first time in a long time, I had a best buddy in town. I had someone with whom I could enjoy girl talk. I could swing by Stacey's house uninvited for a glass of wine or meet up with her at Starbucks for a quick chat after work. We would talk about everything from her dates, her broken family life, Mike's business, to the future. We meshed well, perhaps on an unhealthy level, because we were both unhappy in different ways. She lacked love, support, and security. I lacked peace and confidence. Sadly, a part of me probably felt better about myself because some of what she longed for was what I already had in my life.

I depended on Stacey in many ways, and although she mostly talked about the upheaval in her life, I had secretly hoped to one day rely on her as my confidant. I wanted her to play that role so badly, I found myself subconsciously becoming her provider. Maybe if I do X, she'll give me Y. I probably went overboard in caring for her. A part of me was hoping that in doing so, our friendship would reach a new level where I could share my innermost secrets. I played her savior well, but my actions proved detrimental to our friendship.

Stacey became a fixture in our family, a woman who had problems I was confident I could fix. Like a mother bear, I felt the need to protect her at my expense. Literally. When she told me she was getting married, I felt sorry for her because her relationship with her own family was strained. Her parents weren't thrilled about her fiancé so they cut themselves out of her life. Seeing Stacey having to plan what should have been one of the happiest events in her life by herself crushed me. I rushed in to the rescue, with my trusty cape and my open wallet. I bought her a wedding gown and was a part of her bridal party.

I was also there when Stacey delivered her first child at home, and I even assembled the birthing tub. I bought so much baby stuff for her I was dreaming of cribs, onesies, and Baby Einstein toys for months. When her marriage started to shatter, I was there to help sweep up the broken pieces. I flew in on my white horse of cash and gave her whatever I thought would help her messy situation. I loaned her furniture and helped her finance a car and buy a house. I made sure she always had the money to pay her mortgage payments and added a cell phone to the wish list of stuff I thought she needed in order to survive. I even found a top-of-the-line divorce attorney and loaned her the retainer fee.

And then, through a string of what I believed were God-ordained incidences, I started to see the light. Mike and Stacey were attending an Ali Brown event in Los Angeles one year. He called me one night to ask what I thought of him investing a large sum of money in a mentorship program, a mastermind group of ten like-minded people who want to grow their business to extraordinary levels. At first I balked. We didn't have the money. We barely had enough to pay our personal bills, and my dear husband wanted to take how much and put it in what kind of program?

I remember looking down at my wrist and seeing a bracelet I always wore that read "Live your dreams." I had an epiphany at that moment. I knew if I told Mike "no," then in essence I would be preventing him from fulfilling his dreams. Who was I to stop him from going after what he wanted? What he believed in? What I knew he was ultimately doing to secure a worthwhile future for our family? The last thing I wanted was to hold Mike back.

I said yes. Mike was thrilled but Stacey was floored. She later told me that I had made the biggest mistake of my life. "Mike always puts business before family," she angrily hissed over a telephone call later that night. In hindsight, she used to reiterate that same statement over and over through the years. It was almost like she was trying to paint him as a selfish, cold-hearted man who didn't make his wife or children a priority.

Something clicked when Stacey voiced her disapproval. I knew I had made the right choice. Our relationship began to turn sour.

We ran a marathon in San Diego in June of 2008. It was a taxing race for me because it was where Carol used to live. I needed as much encouragement as possible. I was overly emotional the entire trip and understandably so. Running around the marathon loop brought me face-to-face with coffee bars, clothing stores, and restaurants my sister and I frequented. I almost broke down when I rounded the corner and saw her apartment bordering the race line.

I needed emotional support from Stacey more than ever on those critical days. But relying on her wasn't an option. Whenever I tried to lean on her as a crutch, I fell flat on my face every time. Stacey had started dating a guy and talked about him nonstop. It was like a high school crush and would have been cute, except she bordered on being obsessive.

She spent a good portion of our weekend on the phone with him. Their conversations typically ended in a verbal brawl, with Stacey moaning about what a jerk he was and then checking her Facebook account on her phone to see if he posted anything about her or their latest spat. It was pathetic. Especially because this was behavior coming from a grown woman who was thirty years old.

When I needed Stacey the most, she was too tangled in her own superficial web to even notice I needed her. She was too busy sloppily trying to maneuver around another unhealthy relationship. She was too selfish to see that I was hurting. It pained me to see the ugly truth of our bond, that it wasn't as strong as I had once believed, and I knew there was no way we would resume the closeness we might have once shared.

The fact was, we were growing apart. I was starting to

make some internal changes. I was rediscovering my faith and realizing some of the unhealthy patterns I had established in my life. It was time to break the chains of the past and forge ahead with a new future. I wanted to be healthier, not just physically but emotionally, mentally, and spiritually. And yes, a part of trekking that new journey meant evaluating my relationships. Major change was on its way.

As it turned out, my initial gut call about Stacey not fulfilling her obligations as Mike's employee was right. Though she was a key to the marketing and networking components of the business which was integral to getting and keeping clients, she bailed at most of the events she needed to attend. Stacey would say she couldn't go to such-and-such party or this-and-that workshop because she had to take care of her baby, but we'd later find out she was bar-hopping instead. Also, the part of the business that was her primary obligation wasn't generating income or showing any signs of growth. Mike had no choice but to close down that side of the business and let her go.

I knew about his decision and later I found out Stacey had a feeling the partnership was breaking down and she was going to be ousted from her job. I was there when she walked into Mike's office for what would be the last time. She wasn't in there for more than a few minutes when she walked right out, stunned. She glared at me on her way out the door but didn't say a word. I felt frozen. I didn't know what to say to her. Bye? See you later? Thanks for nothing? You got what you deserve? Good luck?

It only took a few days before a nasty lawsuit ensued between my husband and Stacey. Though he offered her a buyout clause, she refused it and hired an attorney to get her more money. It was a long, nasty, bitter division of business. In my naïveté, I had thought our friendship was strong enough to keep business out of it, but I was wrong. She turned everything into a personal battle.

Stacey had accused my husband of making passes at her when he was drunk. It was baloney and merely another channel she tried to use to finagle more money out of the settlement. Apart from my moments of anger, however, most of all I was hurt. How could someone with whom I had given so much and shared so much turn around and attack me in such a personal way? One thing was certain; I wasn't going to play any role in her nasty game. I tried as best as I could to be cordial, peaceful, and calm whenever she slapped us with yet another dirty legal move or accusation.

It took months, almost a year for me to even consider being friends with anyone else. I always assumed, like I did with my sister, that this friendship would last forever. I took the loss hard. I felt almost the same kind of deep pain I had felt when my sister passed away. It opened up realities in my heart that were painful to face. Like the fact that I was lonely, that I missed my sister, and the question of whether or not I would ever have a best friend again.

You might think it strange, but I still think about Stacey from time to time. In a good way. I certainly don't wish her ill will. I was at an event not too long ago where the bestselling author of *Sex and the City*, Candace Bushnell, was signing books. Stacey is a huge fan of this writer, so I stood in a long line to get a signed copy of her latest book. I'm not sure when, but some day I will give her this gift. And I know it will mean a lot to her.

The forgiveness I was able to give Stacey comes back to the lesson I learned that God puts people into your life for a reason. And it's up to you to learn and grow and better yourself through that experience. I think about it this way. Had it not been for our relationship with her, Mike may not have turned toward the church and we might not have had an amazing relationship with our pastor. So in a weird way, I'm almost grateful that we crossed paths.

❖

I like what Oprah Winfrey once said, "Lots of people want to ride with you in the limo, but what you want is someone who will take the bus with you when the limo breaks down." I've found this to be very true. It's a telling barometer of how genuine a relationship is.

Through my bumps and bruises in finding and cultivating solid relationships, I've learned a few things along the way. I've realized how important it is to connect with people through your belief system. I have rediscovered my faith in the last several years and can see the difference in associating with people who share my core values. I'm not saying I only hang out with people who believe exactly what I do; frankly, I think it's impossible for anyone to share the same thoughts, feelings, ideas, and beliefs. I simply value those who have a similar foundation of beliefs—a faith in God and a desire to nurture a personal relationship with Him, not a cookie-cutter-Sundays-only kind of faith.

I also like having people around me who are positive. Who want to see themselves succeed. Who believe that all things are possible. Who are on a continual journey to better themselves. I find it's these kinds of people who make me want to better myself. Sometimes we have to let go of the negative, energy-sucking relationships that are cluttering our lives and dragging us down and replace them with positive people who are striving for a better life.

The group of women who sit around sipping cappuccinos or wine talking about the latest pair of boots they bought or how their friend's new boob job is outrageous or how much time they spent at the gym over the weekend doesn't quite fit into the vision I have of nurturing, healthy, and worthwhile relationships. It might be okay for some people, but it doesn't work for me.

I am aware of the suspicions I have of people when I meet them for the first time. I know this mistrust comes from the broken friendships of my past. It's not easy to admit, but I'm inclined to make immediate judgments about others, even before I have a chance to get to know them. I scrutinize their every look, every action, and every word that comes out of their mouths to determine if they're sincere or if they want something from me. I know this is not good.

I have to be willing to take a step back and let those who come into my life just be and not judge them based on one encounter. I mean seriously. What if they had a bad day? What if their cat just died? What if they lost their job a week ago? I'm working on giving people the space to be who they are without immediately assuming they are distracted, depressed, snobbish, or that they just don't like me.

Giving has always been an important part of who I am. Yes, I have definitely used this quality to ultimately sabotage or hurt my friendships with others instead of making them better. I've since learned how I can help or bless those in need without enabling them. It took a long time for me to learn this principle.

If someone is in need, I don't hesitate to donate my time, clothes, food, money, whatever it will take to improve their situation. Because I have been blessed in life, I believe in the principle of blessing others. I remember the hard times Mike and I went through trying to start our life. We didn't have much and were fortunate to know generous people who provided us with basic necessities. In a big way, giving is my part in paying it forward.

One of the biggest life lessons I've learned is that it's much better to teach someone how to fish rather than give them the fish. For the longest time—Stacey being one of many examples I could tell you about—I was not only buying friends a fish, I was also cleaning it, gutting it, refrigerating it, and cooking it in a gourmet meal for them.

Within the last few years, I met a woman named Jenn. A friend of ours referred her to us thinking she would be a great asset to our company. Mike and I immediately liked her and hired her to manage our bookkeeping. Jenn had just separated from her abusive husband and was staying with her three children at her sisters' house. She wanted to find her own place to live and I was all too eager to help. Why look, I asked myself, when I could set her up in our empty lake house for a few months? No one was staying there for the winter so it seemed like the perfect solution.

I offered her our cottage free of charge and paid for all utilities like cable, Internet, and electricity. You're probably thinking, "Really, Becky? Again?" Well, now I know I should have handled the situation better, but the truth is I'm a sucker when it comes to children. Jenn had three small babies that needed food and shelter. How could I not provide for them when I already had more than enough?

My intention by helping Jenn was not just to give her money to get spa treatments or go on vacation, but to get her back on her feet. So when she asked us for a $7,000 loan to get situated in her new life apart from her husband, I agreed and drew up a flexible plan for her to repay us.

Not too long after Jenn accepted our loan, she moved back in with her husband. So much for starting a new life. Meanwhile, her work ethic was rapidly declining. When I reviewed the hours she turned in, I knew there was no way she was taking that much time doing what we needed her to do.

She was obviously exaggerating how long she spent working. Projects that should have taken the average person a few hours would take her a few days. She was trying to beef up her paycheck as much as she could, and we had no choice but to let her go. I recently discovered that after reuniting with her husband, Jenn ended up getting a divorce anyway and was back in the same place she started, broke, alone, and without a job.

Instead of giving her everything on a silver platter, I should have given her tools so she could provide for herself. You can't just give people money; you have to teach them how to make it, manage it, and wisely steward it. When life problems come our way, and they always do, sometimes the best thing for us in the long run is to suffer through them instead of being bailed out. How else are we going to learn? How else are we going to be stretched? How else will our character grow?

I wasn't really helping people when I bailed them out. I was just putting a Band-Aid over their wounds, not caring for their wounds but just giving them temporary relief. Bailing people out doesn't do them any service. Helping them develop life survival skills and find inner peace, contentment, and wisdom is what can ultimately help them.

The life lessons I learned in finding true friends paved the way for me to help my daughter in her tug-of-war trying to build a solid network of friends. In high school, her peers cruelly nicknamed Sara "Rich Bitch." They see her as being able to afford expensive things and they don't like it. They talk behind her back, tease her, and make fun of her saying things like, "Daddy will give the little Miss Princess whatever she wants."

Just as adults make premature assumptions and judgments about others, teens do the same thing. My girl has had many friendships destroyed because of those assumptions and it provoked her to fall into a depression.

I'm trying my best to teach Sara the same lessons I've learned. I'm trying my best to help her stay grounded, befriend peers who love her just the way she is, and distance herself from those who are jealous, cruel, and vindictive. It's not an easy task. I just hope she takes these lessons into adulthood and does a better job than I did of cultivating lasting friendships that revolve around more than money or petty stuff.

For the last few years, school has been rough for Sara. She has been the victim of relentless bullying from mean girls. You have to know some things about my daughter. She works. She doesn't sit around watching TV while the maid cleans her room. She also just smashed up her clunker and has to buy another car with her own money. And she'll still have to pay for her own car insurance and gas, too. But Sara's classmates don't know that about her.

They assume the princess needs to get off her high horse. This is the same "princess" who used to drive a 2003 Trailblazer with the front bumper held in place by chicken wire. The same princess who studies until the wee hours of the morning to maintain her straight-A average. The same princess who runs half marathons to raise money for the Leukemia and Lymphoma Society. The same princess who struggles with being a people-pleaser and spends many after school hours tutoring her classmates.

I think about the challenges I've had finding and nurturing friendships in a healthy and life-giving way and the loneliness it has caused in me. I think about the challenges my daughter faces in feeling depressed and anxious because of the cruel antics the girls at school play at her expense. Both situations overwhelm me. I know a lot of my insecurities in relationships stem from self-doubt, from always second-guessing myself to believing that I'm not enough, and I see pieces of those same haunting ghosts in my daughter.

For me, it feels like I'm at the bottom of the stairs again, sitting underneath a pile of eggshells I'm trying so hard not to break, waiting for my mom to calm down so I can try to fix her sadness. It's not a good place to be. Not for me or for my daughter. But for years I was there. And for years I allowed life to pass me by like I was watching a big screen movie while paralyzed by insecurities. When you don't believe in yourself, it's hard to believe in anything.

5
When I Stopped Believing in Me

"No one can make you feel inferior without your consent."
~ Eleanor Roosevelt

“*I* don't know how to be happy.” It's a statement you may have heard from one of your friends, a co-worker, maybe you've even said it yourself at some point. It's normal, isn't it? Who's not unhappy at least at some point in life? Who's not bored in their marriage? Or dissatisfied with their career? Or frustrated with the pounds they've recently packed on? Who doesn't get in a funk just because they woke up on the wrong side of the bed?

But when my sixteen-year-old daughter uttered those words, I took special notice. It broke my heart. A heavy sadness coated Sara's beautiful chocolate brown eyes and shadowed her typically cheery expression. “I don't know how to be happy,” she repeated. I could feel the burden that weighed heavily on her shoulders. The weight of depression. The weight of doubt. The weight of tears that don't ever seem to go away.

As a parent, your instinct is to shield your kids from tough times but when you can't, you want desperately to fix whatever pain they endure. But this wasn't something I could fix. I couldn't slap a Band-Aid on my daughter's achy heart. I could only get her into therapy.

I had one advantage in helping her—I could definitely relate on some level to what she was going through. Still, I never had those feelings until I was in my thirties, and our discontent sprung from different origins. While my lack of happiness stemmed from wanting more out of life, her lack of happiness was just life. It was an empty feeling. A pit. I did notice a similarity between her and my mom's illness. The parallel was disturbing.

While Sara's confession didn't shock me, it pained me because she had struggled with internal issues for about six years. Her statement was a blaring red light that it was getting worse. Sara saw her first therapist in the fifth grade and was diagnosed with situational depression based on what was going on in her class, that she was being bullied by her class-mates. Yes, that's right. The good old-fashioned Catholic school she attended, the one that we hoped would save Sara from the perils of public school, had a fair share of mean girls. These bullies sent her mean messages and called her fat and other derogatory terms that made me angry.

Sara would get off the bus at the end of the day and cry for hours. Nothing I did would calm her down. And sadly, with four other kids to take care of, it was a challenge to give her undivided attention, the attention she probably needed at the time.

My daughter shared with me that at one point, she had a knife to her wrist and was tempted to use it. But Sara knew she would likely cry out from the pain, and that noise would likely alarm me, and I'd likely save her in the nick of time, and then she would not only still be here having to face her depression but she would also get into trouble. Having me reprimand her for a suicide attempt was ridiculous, but that's what my sweet girl believed. I'm glad she never followed through. I don't know what I would have done.

Sara's teacher told me, "It's God's will for Sara to go through this" (meaning the bullying). I took my cue and enrolled my daughter elsewhere. While this woman's comment made me seethe with rage and tempted me to shake her like a rag doll by her starchy habit, I can now see that it was a wakeup call for me. A divine one at that.

It was time to pull my daughter out of school and get us both educated on depression. I knew there was a long road ahead of us. Over the years she went to numerous therapists. Some helped; others weren't so good. When she would come home from a session and tell me how frustrated she was because she didn't think "it was working," I noted the irony. My mother used to say the same thing when my dad sent her from one doctor to another. Granted doctors back in the day weren't as well schooled on debilitating mental health issues as they are today, but there were some great psychiatrists available.

When I would tell my daughter to just continue doing what she was doing and hang in there, she'd bark at me in a classic snarky teenage attitude way (with a little whine on the side) and say, "You just don't understand, Mom." That's how I knew the therapy was working, because she was acting like a regular adolescent, not like a walking zombie.

Having Sara combat her struggles brought attention to my own. For so many years I spent my time, energy, and efforts trying to make everyone else happy but I couldn't find even an ounce of happiness in myself. I should have won awards for people-pleasing, I was so good. I thought if everyone else was happy, life would be a-okay. If my kids were happy, there'd be peace at home. If Mike was happy, our finances would be steady and stable. If my parents were happy, I could be the good daughter.

I worried about everything all the time and wanted desperately to please the microcosm around me and the macrocosm of the big world out there. I hoped it would ease my anxiety. Unlike Sara, depression wasn't an issue with me; anxiety was my problem. If I could make a situation better, I would do it. I took care of everyone around me and neglected myself along the way. It got worse when Mike started his own business. He always had the "play big to win" attitude and he was definitely living his philosophy.

But before our finances leveled off to a comfortable position, our debt was piling up. As the numbers went up, my anxiety went up. No matter what we did, it seemed we were just borrowing from Peter to pay Paul. Bills freaked me out. Living expenses freaked me out. I'd lay awake at night wondering what I could do to ease the financial burden, worrying about how it would affect our children and wondering if money would one day completely disappear.

I worried about everything. My weight. My health. My children. My marriage. The finances. When I wasn't worrying, I was fixing everyone else's problems and making them happy. It was the only thing that afforded me temporary peace. The anxiety plus my penchant to people-please was a coupling that ultimately sabotaged me on the inside and on the outside. By the time I realized I had no happy place to call my own for these reasons, I had already spent years unknowingly being pummeled by self-doubt.

Self-doubt was a looming issue I wrestled with for years. It's one of the main reasons I landed in therapy three years ago and goes hand-in-hand with the anxiety. While on one hand,

I was able to laugh at myself for doing something silly or stupid like trip or mispronounce a word; on the other hand, deep down I felt overweight, fashion-illiterate, and purposeless.

The weight issue was a big deal. Five babies will wreak havoc on your body. No doubt about that. I wouldn't trade any amount of pounds for my beautiful children, but seeing my body change in ways I couldn't keep up with chipped away at my self-esteem. But here's the funny thing. Even when I lost weight between babies three and four, I still wasn't happy.

So I started experimenting. I started doing things to mask my insecurities and the truth of what was going on inside of me. I tried hair extensions. I tried makeup. I tried jewelry. I turned into a fashion wannabe. I loved browsing through fashion and beauty magazines and admiring the beautiful women photographed on the pages. I wanted to look like them. Maybe that would supercharge my spirit and make me feel good. Or worthy. Or enough. Isn't that what we all just want to feel?

News flash. Even when I adorned myself with pretty jewels and couture dresses, I may have looked fabulous on the outside, but I still felt nothing on the inside. I felt like there was a black hole in my heart. I was paralyzed and couldn't understand why I was so good at helping everyone else, but I sucked at believing in myself and believing in the best for my life. The obvious was sobering. I was crippling myself through gaining weight, being fearful, and by allowing stress to abort any forward movement to better myself.

Much of my self-doubt issues stemmed from my body image and the increasing number on my scale as our family unit grew bigger. In high school and college, I was active and very competitive. I played basketball and ran track and field. I was always thin and probably even a little too thin in high school when I was exercising almost every day. But I never thought about my weight. I was never concerned about my body image. I never compared myself to the girls in school or to movie stars on TV. My body simply wasn't an issue.

Aside from my mother's mental illness, I felt I was raised to be a confident young woman. My father believed in empowering me with education and athletic skill. He wanted me to be strong and independent, traits I easily developed. My dad was always complimentary and I felt loved and secure. He'd shower me with sincere praise and never stopped hammering into my head how smart, good, and pretty he thought I was.

I don't remember him ever being mad at me. I think he may have spanked me once when my brother and I knocked over and broke my sister's lamp while jumping on the bed. My dad stopped the spanking business after he tried to whack my brother on the bottom but instead of crying, my brother laughed. I think that humiliated my dad so much he never spanked us again.

When I started dating Mike, I was introduced to the blue collar world. My social circle was refined and sophisticated due to my father's mingling with the upper echelon at the university; Mike's circle was laid back and loose. His family and friends seldom cared about what came out of their mouths; I heard them say some pretty inappropriate and uncouth things. Mike's dad was driving us somewhere when we passed a billboard on the highway that showed an attractive young woman sprawled over a fancy red car. My future father-in-law made a comment that made me blush. I felt uncomfortable as I squirmed in the backseat trying hard to hide my embarrassment.

Mike's college buddies were the same way. They constantly talked about women. And not just any woman. They hailed women who were thin and had long, flowing blonde hair and huge breasts that could easily pass the pencil test. They constantly made comments about how hot that celebrity, Playboy or super model was while bashing women who didn't fit into this unrealistic mold. It was then I started being conscious of my own body. Was I too tall? Was I maybe a little chubby? Was I one of the fat girls they made fun of?

Once I started having kids, my body image anxiety took on a whole other level. When I was pregnant with Sara, I was working for a boss who didn't have any kids. Her boss also didn't have children and neither did that man's boss. So the management team couldn't understand or even try to sympathize with the idiosyncrasies of being pregnant. Not that I expected special treatment, mind you.

I was just frustrated because of the demand on me to put in over fifty hours of work a week and bring home a forty-hour paycheck. I was never a strict nine-to-five girl. Never have been and never will be. I never watched the clock or punched out exactly on time because I just wanted to go home. I loved working; putting in extra hours to finish whatever needed to get done didn't concern me one bit. So their approach to demand extra time was irritating and made me feel like a little kid. The situation stressed me out; I coped by indulging my tendency to overeat.

During my pregnancy, I chunked out and gained about fifty pounds. It was the first time I ever gained a massive amount of weight. And it didn't look like it would stop any time soon. Before Taylor was born, I was already carrying an extra thirty or forty pounds and gained another twenty pounds. I was right back where I was when Sara was born.

When Brendan, baby number three, came along, my anxiety was at an all-time high because Mike was starting his new career and our financial situation was shaky. Well, more than shaky; we had no money. I already had two kids at home and couldn't work because my paycheck wouldn't cover the daycare costs. I was trying to play the role of Happy Homemaker while pretending not to worry. I was eating like crap because we could only afford cheap food, which is usually processed, packed with sugar, and fattening. Being put on bed rest because of preeclampsia toward the end of my pregnancy didn't help matters, either.

The shining light in this dark tunnel was that during the pregnancy I was working out and even got certified as an aerobic instructor before I was diagnosed with preeclampsia. Those were the days when women wore high-cut unitards and tights. But even though my outfits were unforgiving for a pregnant woman who had a couple of extra pounds on her, I had tons of fun and started to feel better about myself.

After I gave birth, the pounds peeled right off. I was at my goal weight, but surprise, surprise, I wasn't happy. I thought seeing that perfect number on my scale would be akin to finding the Holy Grail. Not so much. And getting to that goal weight was torture. I ate nothing but Slim-Fast shakes and a nasty green diet drink that tasted like swamp water and promised me a dream body but not much else.

When I finally made it to my ideal size, I waited for my life to drastically change. I waited for the fireworks. The red carpet. The confetti. The popping of a champagne cork and the raising of glasses. Nothing. So I continued to wait for about a month, still anticipating my invitation to the party welcoming me into a new dream life, but guess what? There was no party. There was no celebration. There was nothing but the same old me and a number on the scale innocently blinking back at me.

I still didn't feel good about myself. I still didn't think I was enough.

Then I got pregnant and gave birth to Morgan. The pounds were back with a vengeance. They missed me, they said. And they relentlessly wooed me with Big Macs and French fries. I swear there is something in that special sauce that makes pregnant women go nuts. As they whispered sweet nothings into my ear, the food and extra weight convinced me that I deserved these indulgences because, as they not so delicately put it, my life sucked. Now did it really suck? No, but I was so miserable and wrought with anxiety and self-doubt that I couldn't see much of the good.

Here I was with four children under the age of seven. While motherhood was rewarding in unbelievable ways, I couldn't quash my anxious feelings about not being completely fulfilled apart from raising my kids. I had nothing of my own, no hobbies, no favorite thing to do, nothing. And I was a hot mess. Mike would come home from work around eight in the evening and I looked like a wreck. I was tired. I was dirty. I smelled.

When my doctor diagnosed me with post partum depression after Morgan was born, I looked at him numbly and nodded at his conclusion. "Well, I haven't slept in twelve years. Maybe that's why I don't feel so good." Physically, my body was kaput. I was exhausted. I was not taking care of myself and honestly, a big part of me didn't feel like it was right to invest in "me" time, whether it was taking time to exercise, spending money on and cooking healthier meals, or even taking a twenty minute bubble bath. If I took time for me, life as I know it would stop, right? What about the kids? What about Mike? What about my parents? What about the laundry? Or the bills? For Pete's sake, how will the earth rotate on its axis without my help?

My weight gain made me feel pretty bad about myself. It didn't help that my husband had good-looking women working for him (yes, I hired them). I wasn't threatened by them, I was jealous. And I wasn't entirely jealous of their good looks. I was also jealous of my husband. I was jealous that Mike was on a particular quest and he was going to do whatever it took to achieve it.

While I wasn't yet sure how to incorporate more meaning or purpose in my life outside of motherhood, there was one thing I could immediately set out to do—lose weight. So I hightailed it to the bookstores, to my doctor, to weight clinics, and to support groups. I did Weight Watchers, Jenny Craig, NutriSystem, and tried Slim-Fast again. I went diet bonkers. I spent a few weeks eating non-fat crap that tasted like cardboard smothered in condiments that failed to mask the nastiness. I would lose a few pounds but wouldn't you know it, a few weeks after that, I'd gain it all back. I tried walking with a neighbor, which did help ignite a little weight loss, and then I found out I was pregnant with Madison.

My weight issues had me in a headlock. It was a vicious game. If I ate something unhealthy, I would run to the scale to see if I had gained a pound or I would try not to eat for the rest of the day to make up for screwing up. I hated going to Mike's company events or meetings because I didn't look like most of the other wives. They were thin; I was fat. They had their place in their social cliques; I was desperately trying to fit in. They looked like Barbie dolls; the best I could do was dress myself in something that camouflaged my weight and wasn't stained with children's poop, vomit, or spit up.

I felt defeated in so many areas, particularly my weight. Despite repeatedly giving it the good old college try—experimenting with new diets and even going to doctors to see if I had a medical condition—I could not lose the weight. One day Mike gave me a hug and reassured me that I was doing the best I could. "You're trying, Becky. I know you are. I can see that."

But here's the kicker. I'm smart enough now to know that extra pounds don't make or break a woman. It's about finding contentment and peace even if the pounds aren't dropping or the dress is a little snug. It's hard to find that inner harmony when we are judged all the time, either by the media, society, or even by strangers or our loved ones. But who cares, right? I mean, who really cares what people think?

As much as I hate to admit it, I did and it was because I didn't love myself. I hid behind my extra weight because I had no self-love. I loved my husband, my children, and my parents so much that I didn't have any love leftover for myself. So even when I lost the weight and looked thinner, I still didn't like myself. The change wasn't anything but a topical transformation.

Being skinny, being fat, it doesn't make a difference. Our body image and overall confidence is not found in what we look like or how others perceive us. It's found in how we love ourselves. It's found when we stop doubting ourselves. When we stop feeling less than. When we stop feeling like we don't measure up. When we stop feeling inadequate.

I remember sitting outside and watching my daughter and her girlfriends play in the pool. In the midst of the idle chatter, laughter, and splashing, I heard them say things that broke my heart. One girl would complain to the others, "I'm so fat." Another would sound off, "I wish I was pretty." On and on it went. I thought to myself, "Who is teaching these beautiful teen girls to doubt themselves so much?" And then I realized that we, their parents, are when we say those things about ourselves.

I constantly strive every day to tell my daughters how beautiful they are. I remind them that there is nothing that they cannot do. I teach them to treat others like they would want to be treated. And through these things, I hope they can learn to love and believe in themselves so they don't have the struggles I had.

☙

The one area where I had total confidence was in being a mother. Whenever I talked about my children, my shoulders settled, my muscles relaxed, and I breathed more easily. I was a loving, caring mother who continued to do her best to create a peaceful environment for her babies.

Being a wife, however, was a different story. My biggest area of weakness was in not taking care of myself and not communicating with my husband about my needs. Because I felt poorly on the inside, I bottled up my voice. Sure, I was a supportive wife and Mike knew he could count on me to encourage him, believe in him, and independently maneuver through the ins and outs of our family so he could follow and live out his dreams. But in doing so, I lost a part of my true self.

I was petrified to rock the boat by piping up about something or giving an opinion I felt I needed to give or by doing the wrong thing, which was anything other than what my husband wanted. I definitely did not want to stifle Mike's dream because he was on such a great path. I thought any differing opinion I gave would warrant him leaving me and I had a deep-rooted fear of being alone. Merely thinking about saying or doing something that would unsettle our otherwise peaceful relationship could easily trigger a panic attack.

I lived anticipating the worst many times and ran my brain crazy asking "What if" questions. What if we didn't get a paycheck? What if I would never lose the weight? What if we couldn't pay the house bill? What if my parents were mad at me? I've since learned you can't live by the *what ifs* in life. Hypotheticals can't give me a life that is worth living.

Doubt and negativity is something that many people struggle with. I heard that 70% of our thoughts are negative. Can you imagine how much better we would feel about ourselves, our lives, and our future if that 70% was positive? We'd make such a difference in this world.

Running was one way I could clear my head, at least temporarily, from the negative thinking. When I started running in 2005, I thought I was working on myself. And in a way, I was. But I also hoped running would help nudge my weight loss forward. So I did like Forest Gump and ran like crazy. In fact, I ran nine half marathons and three marathons in one year alone. You know what happened? I transferred my compulsive behavior to people-please and my desire for "something" into overtraining. All this did was compound my stress. So even though I put my body to the test and burned what seemed like a million calories a day, I was exhausting myself and eating more than I should have. I ended up gaining weight.

Still, I learned a lot from running. I found out I could do something for myself. I could be competitive. I could win. I could achieve something. It was a stepping stone that would leave me with more than fancy ribbons and plenty of fancy medals. It would lead me into finding my way.

It was another step forward. I like what Anne Lamott writes in the opening of her book *Traveling Mercies*. She describes her soul conversion not as one grand event, but as a "series of staggers" from one place to the next, ultimately bringing her closer to belief. I think that's the case for many of us when we are on a quest for transformation. We usually don't get from point A to point B in one shot; it usually takes us circling around the entire alphabet until we get to the end. I know that's how transformation came to me.

6
Running to Stand Still

"The miracle isn't that I finished. The miracle is that
I had the courage to start."

~ John Bingham

It's that temporary lull of the day when the house seems unusually but refreshingly quiet. The kids are in their rooms—maybe doing homework, more than likely playing a video game or watching TV—and you realize that for however long the mysterious calm lasts, you have peace and quiet. Peace and quiet is a luxury that most moms don't get, so if we're smart, we take advantage of that time.

I use those few precious moments to lock myself in the bathroom. And why wouldn't I? It's the most private place in the house. It's just me, the toilet, the sink, and the bathtub. I take a deep breath in, oblivious of the mayhem that an ordinary day brings, and exhale. And then...like clockwork...

It starts.

"Mom! Moooooooom!" There is a slight pause. Silence. I don't hear my name being yelled at the top of one of my children's lungs. I pray I won't have to hear it for at least ten more minutes. That's all I ask for. Ten minutes.

No such luck.

"Mooooommmmmm!" This time the voice screams bloody murder. Which usually means this one hit that one, or this one ate that one's sandwich, or this one is watching one show and that one wants to watch another one. You know what I'm describing, major "I-need-Mom-and-I-need-her-now" drama! My lull is officially shattered.

This scenario is one of the reasons I started running. I wanted to get away from it all for a few minutes. I wanted to listen to birds chirping, waves lapping onto the shore, even speeding cars and trucks whizzing by, anything except the shrilling cry of a child who thinks an empty peanut butter jar constitutes an emergency.

Like any mother, I needed some time to myself where I could de-stress, get rejuvenated, and have time to unwind. Having at least a little bit of "me time" makes every woman a better wife and mother. Running kept me busy and equalized my sanity for thirty minutes or an hour. It was my sacred time. I didn't care if I was choking down exhaust as I ran on the side of the highway; it was still my sacred time.

There's another reason I started running, a simple one. I realized my long walks were taking too long. If I ran, I could be home twice as fast. But it was a catch-22. The longer I walked, the greater the chance for my kids to call me on my cell phone to ask for something ("Where are my soccer cleats?") or to complain about one of their siblings misbehaving ("Sara tried to stick a frog down my shirt!"). If I picked up my pace though, "me time" would be shortened, and I wouldn't have as many distractions.

Once I started gaining more speed, I noticed I was losing weight and certain areas on my body stopped jiggling so much. It was then I officially became addicted. Having alone time to think, solve problems, and come up with ideas plus the added bonus of shedding unwanted pounds was a divine coupling. Running was the Romeo to my Juliet.

The love affair aside, let me get one thing straight. While I was smitten with my newfound activity and loved what it did for me, I didn't entirely like running for the mere fact that I hate to sweat. Running makes me sweat. A lot. Still, there is nothing like the feeling of satisfaction you get when you finish a run and know that you pounded out your projected goal, mile after mile, sweat-drenched body and all. I suppose there are plusses and minuses to everything.

I loved what running afforded me. It gave me relief to know I was working on my weight issues. It gave me purpose to know I was doing something worthwhile. It gave me the feeling that I wasn't so bad after all and maybe, just maybe, I was enough. Most importantly, running brought to mind that God was always with me. Looking back at all the races I completed, I can connect the dots and see how God used certain places, people, and things to show me He is actively involved in my life and there is significance to my existence.

I started with a couple of 5K races to get motivated before I signed up for longer races. After doing a handful of three-milers, I decided they were too short. Here's what I mean. The first mile is like a warm up, the second mile is where I start to feel good, and by the third mile, I'm in my groove and ready to rock and roll, but then POOF! There's the finish line and the race is over, just when I start to feel like a rock star.

So I upped my game and signed up for a 10K. That was a mistake. Those races are for the 5K superstars. I did my first 10K in May of 2005 and finished just as the sponsors and volunteers were tearing down the race signs and banners and were ready to call it a day. I was pregnant with Madison so I did pretty well considering my body was in baby-making mode.

I conquered that 10K, decided that was enough and moved to my next challenge, the half marathon. I had run the Bayshore half marathon when I was pregnant with Madison. Well, I power walked most of it, I was so exhausted. The first half marathon that I felt good running was at Disneyland in 2007. That race was magical. The weather was perfect. Running in balmy weather with the sun on your back is surprisingly motivating, as were the Disney characters lined up on the sides of the race, cheering the runners on as we booked it through the park. Winnie the Pooh and friends gave us high-fives along the way. Ariel and Goofy gave us water as we raced by. Track suit-wearing Mickey and Minnie Mouse jumped up and down for us at the finish line. Although it was a race, many partici-pants stopped in the middle of running and had their pictures taken with the Disney celebrities. That was one race I could have run forever...okay, maybe not forever, but definitely longer than thirteen miles.

Here's what I learned about these longer races—there's a prize to look forward to at the end. A real prize. Everyone who runs in a marathon gets a medal. Everyone! It doesn't matter if it takes you two hours to run it or two days, you still get a shiny, gold parting gift for completing a half or full marathon. My home office showcases a whole shelf dedicated to my 25 plus medals. They're heavy, they're big, and they mean a lot more to me than just stepping over a line. To me, they repre-sent the magic I was missing. I can look at that shelf even today and feel proud of myself.

The medal system was my motivation to keep signing up for marathon after marathon. When I heard about the Rock-n-Roll Marathon Series, I got even more pumped up. This series offers half and full marathons across the country with live music, post race concerts, and the most spirited spectators. Running two races in the series earns a third bonus medal. Running three earns another bonus one. You know how many medals you get when you keep running these sponsored marathons? A whole lot. My eye was on the mac daddy Superman medal, the one you get by running seven Rock-n-Roll races, including two full marathons, in a calendar year. The prize was four times the size of a regular medal and decorated with sparkles and bling. The first time I saw that beauty, it took my breath away. I wanted one. Nothing would keep me away from the mac daddy prize which I finally got in 2008.

In 2007, I ran three more half marathons plus one full one in Detroit, which was one of my toughest races. I was feeling under the weather as I geared up at the starting line. I felt dizzy and faint, a prediction that something was physically off. I forged ahead anyway, forcing myself with every bit of strength to put one shoe in front of the other and keep going toward the finish line. I was never able to achieve a rhythm, so I bumbled my way through the miles.

I blame my stomach. A good chunk of my time was spent visiting the porta-potties. My tummy was a wreck from whatever I had eaten the night before and I puked my way through the entire race. Run. Puke. Run. Puke. Twenty-six miles of those two activities does not equal a fun race. But hey, I finished and nothing, not even a queasy stomach, could take away the pride I felt when my sneaker touched down over the finish line.

Walking through the airport on my way home, I was quite a spectacle. I was hobbling around because my legs were so sore. I was also trying hard to create some space between my chafed armpits and my torso, which was raw and bleeding from having my jogging bra dig deep into my chest. The friction of my skin against any surface, even a thin layer of clothes, caused me pain. But I wasn't a sight for sore eyes just because I was walking funny. In addition to my huge purse and carry on bag, I proudly wore the shiny medal on my chest. While I was proud to display proof of my accomplishment, it also helped tell the story of why I was walking so strangely.

The following year, I did eleven races including two marathons. My first race was a part of the Rock-n-Roll series and was held in Phoenix. I was nervous. The race was packed with more people running in it than there are people in my hometown during the winter. I was in the middle of a swarm of people. I couldn't see anything ahead of me except a sea of colorful tank tops and visors. Looking behind me, to the right, and to the left was more of the same, runners wearing bright attire and sporting paper numbers pinned to their tops. I felt like an ant in the middle of an anthill.

My heart was racing and I was already sweating from my worked up nerves. I had never in my life seen so many people doing the same thing I was, running 26 miles to a finish line. And there were so many different kinds of runners. There were serious ones who had focused gazes as they jumped up and down warming up their lean, long limbs. There were fun runners, laughing, horse playing with their friends, and decked out in costumes and balloons tied down to their clothes; they obviously cared more about having a good time than being the fastest or beating the runner next to them. I liked this group the best.

Running with so many people ensured I would not finish last. Knowing I wouldn't be the slowest tempered my anxiety. I was also grateful for the horde of runners because I'd always have someone running with me. I didn't have to necessarily chat up the runner to my left or right, but it was comforting to know I had the option. It was comforting just to know I'd never be alone.

The enthusiasm and partying that goes on at the end of these Rock-n-Roll races gave me an adrenaline rush. I felt like I was walking on cloud nine for hours. This three-day event was exactly what I needed to jumpstart my sluggish energy; I fed off of the rush from the moment I finished the race. I was part of the greatest party on earth and snagged a medal, too. I had a few days away from my family and was able to take a bath and go to the bathroom without any interruptions from screaming kids.

In 2009, I started to downsize and only ran in two marathons and a half marathon.

When Stacey and I were friends, she used to join me in my races because I was afraid to go by myself. I didn't have the confidence to trek out to some unknown city and deal with the nuances of races on my own. Knowing I had a chaperon who could figuratively hold my hand through the process bolstered my confidence.

But we had different running styles. I was a recreational runner and simply finishing a race made me happy. Stacey was forever trying to beat her time. Her mentality was, if I wasn't getting faster, why continue to race? Running came easily for my size two friend. So easily, in fact, that she never cared about the medals. Sometimes I wonder if she felt pressure to run a fast race since she spent a lot of money on them. Maybe she thought the money wouldn't be well spent unless she was satisfied with her time. Who knows?

Whenever we'd finish a race, Stacey would throw her medal in her suitcase. I, on the other hand, would gently caress mine as if it were a rare diamond, then carefully wrap it up in expensive tissue paper, and place it in my carry-on bag so I'd have it with me at all times. Every ten minutes or so I'd unzip my bag and sneak a peek inside to make sure my treasure was still there. I had worked hard for it and I was going to guard it with my life. To Stacey, it was nothing but a cheap trinket, a worthless tchotchke you'd find at a garage sale.

The last time she and I ran together I had an epiphany about running. Stacey chucked her medal in her suitcase, but it plunked down to the floor instead of into its intended target. The shiny object lay there all night, looking haphazardly out of place and alone on the cold floor. I'm pretty sure I heard it say, "Pick me up. Care about me. Treat me right." Stacey's nonchalant attitude sparked in me a different kind of passion for running; I realized that I didn't ever want to run with that kind of attitude.

I never wanted to finish a race and act like it was pointless unless I ran faster than the race before. I wanted running to mean something. I wanted it to be fun and not about being as fast as possible. I wanted to look at a medal I earned with pride and appreciate it as a token of my hard work. I wanted to enjoy myself and not stress whenever I looked at the numbers on the clock.

I ran the San Francisco Nike Women's Marathon in 2008 around my birthday. That particular race was "the" race, at least for me. Instead of a medal for finishing, there was something even better, a silver Tiffany pendant inscribed with the image of two women running. Firefighters wearing tuxedos handed out the signature blue box wrapped in a white ribbon. The race was so popular, there was a lottery drawing to get in. I wanted to increase my chances, so I strategically applied under my name as well as under my alias, S. Rebecca Reese, which was my daughter Sara's name. I didn't think she would mind me using her name for a good cause.

Wouldn't you know it; both names won the lottery as well

as Stacey's. Since Sara was joining us on the trip, I told Stacey she should bring a friend. She brought along a spunky, friendly, and highly intelligent woman named Sherry. Because we were celebrating another year in my life, Sara made plans for us to go on a shopping excursion and Stacey wanted us to get dressed up and enjoy an elaborate dinner. I was excited for this girl's trip and was looking forward to having a "me" day. The trip turned out nothing like I imagined.

Stacey was once again glued to Facebook about some guy. Her obsession threw a wrench into most of the activities planned for that weekend. She was more interested in cyber stalking the guy she was dating than spending time with the rest of us. I spent hours waiting for her in the lobby while she was holed up in her room talking to her boyfriend or checking Facebook.

Sara was also doing her own thing. She would have cheerleading tryouts the day we got back to Michigan, so she spent every possible moment doing cartwheels, handsprings, and air splits whenever space permitted. Sherry and I spent a lot of time together, however, forming a friendship that would unexpectedly connect us in a God-orchestrated way in the future.

At the last possible minute, Sherry decided to run with us, though she was unregistered. Her plan was to hop out of the race a few blocks before the finish line. I was thrilled. She seemed like me in that she just wanted to have a good time running, not be overly competitive. Stacey took off as soon as she heard the gun go off. The three of us remained behind, running together at a leisurely pace. When we finally got into a groove and had more room around us, Sara busted out her cheerleading exercises. She jumped over the cones that were placed on the side of the road and even managed to get in a few cartwheels in between very annoyed runners. We had such a great time even though people made some nasty comments about Sara being distracting with her clowning around. It made for a good laugh for both Sherry and me.

I'm sure if I hadn't horsed around as much, I probably would have run a faster time. But it didn't matter. Having fun was what counted and I accomplished that goal hands down. Sherry ran off the road about five feet away from the finish line, where the city's firefighters dressed in tuxedos held the beautiful boxes of wrapped Tiffany necklaces on silver trays. I'll never forget that race. I got a Tiffany necklace, had fun, and made a new friend. How much better could it have gotten?

❧

I had a turning point when I decided to run the Rock-n-Roll Series Mardi Gras marathon in New Orleans in the beginning of 2010. I didn't know what was happening at the time, but it seemed everything happened to prevent me from running in that event. I believe there was so much resistance because that race would change my life. I've found that when we are supposed to be upleveled in a particular area, there is a lot of stretching of character, growing pains, and discomfort that comes before we get where we are meant to go.

Before I signed up for the race, I felt a gnawing in my gut to call Sherry. I had met and hung out with her two years earlier at the marathon, but I thought about her from time to time. I liked her. She also shared many of the same beliefs I had. It's hard to find someone to talk with about faith and I appreciated that about her. We actually went to the same church, but because it was so big we rarely ran into each other.

Pursuing her friendship was awkward, however, because she was Stacey's friend first. I knew Stacey needed someone like Sherry to support her during the breakdown of her relationship with Mike, but I too wanted to be a part of Sherry's life. I just didn't know how that would look like in light of her ties to Stacey.

It was weird. The feeling of wanting to connect with Sherry was something I just couldn't shake. I hadn't talked to her in a few months but something inside kept telling me to invite her to do something together. Here's the crazy part. I didn't know it then, but Sherry was getting a similar message in her gut. She later shared with me that she had told her husband she felt she needed to do something with me, and that if by chance I called and invited her out, she'd say yes. Her husband encouraged her to follow her intuition.

For a few days I ignored the badgering in my spirit to pick up the phone and dial Sherry's digits. Every time her image came to my mind, I replaced it with something else, like my overwhelming to-do list. But when the thoughts became obsessive I knew one of two things was true. Either, one, she was on my mind for a reason and I had to stop being a baby and just call her or, two, I was plain going crazy. I didn't want to believe I was a kook, so I finally reached out to Sherry. And, boy, was I glad I did.

I asked her if she'd be willing to go with me to New Orleans to cheer me on while I ran in a marathon. She laughed and told me how she'd been thinking of me and had a feeling I'd be calling. It's funny. Sherry imagined I would be calling to ask her to join me in a women's church retreat, one she didn't want to attend. Thankfully, I didn't invite her there, but on an out-of-state weekend trip. "You threw me for a loop," she said and happily agreed to accompany me.

Right before I got off the phone with her, however, after some rethinking on her part, she backed out of the trip because she realized it would cost her more than she could afford. She promised to call me back to confirm. My heart sank. I was disappointed. I thought this was supposed to be an otherworldly connection. Something that was meant to be. Was I totally off my rocker? I could have sworn God was in the middle of this. What I didn't know was that while I was questioning my gut, Sherry's husband was pointing out that our connection just had to have been divinely ordained and this was one invitation she could not refuse. She called right back and said yes.

I had the perfect plan. I booked us a great first-class flight and a fabulous hotel and was pleased with the ideal weather we'd be expecting. It didn't take long for my expectations and perfect plans to shatter. It started snowing heavily when we got to the airport. Though winter snow is certainly not an anomaly where we live, it was unexpected on that particular day. Meteorologists predicted a sunny day without a cloud in the sky. It's funny how things can change on a dime.

Because of the bad weather, all outgoing flights were delayed and we missed our Detroit connection to New Orleans. I freaked. It was Friday and we were scheduled to come back on Sunday, so I wasn't sure if it was even worth going at that point. What if we made it to Detroit only to find out our next flight was delayed or even canceled due to the same snowstorm? What if we got snowed out the entire weekend? What if x? What if y? What if z? Blah, blah, blah. This time, I didn't let my *what ifs* stop me from taking a chance. We ended up hopping on a late flight to Detroit, knowing we might be flying there only to have to take a return flight back to Traverse City that same night.

We did miss our flight to New Orleans and had to spend the night in Detroit because all flights out of that airport were canceled. But we weren't dispirited. There were two silver linings. My credit card company booked us into a great hotel that night and we had a surprise guest join us—my husband.

Mike was flying in from Kansas City that evening, so he was grounded as well. The three of us had a blast catching up in the hotel lounge as we indulged in delicious wine and laughed about the dents in our plans that were out of our control.

Sherry and I made it to New Orleans the next day. She had a pretty heart-stirring plane trip. It was another example of how something was happening in the supernatural realm; it wasn't just my overactive imagination. The flight was packed except for a single seat next to Sherry. A woman seated on the other side of her leaned over and said, "Isn't it funny how God works?" If you have flown for a long time, you know that most passengers don't talk to one another outside of the usual asking someone to move so they can get to the bathroom. And even fewer people mention something about God. It rarely happens unless you are sitting next to a religious nut who makes it her business to convert everyone she meets. The woman seated near Sherry was definitely spiritual. She happened to be a missionary from Africa, but she was far from a nut.

The two women talked about God the entire flight. The missionary had missed her friend's wedding because of the delay and wondered if there was a mysterious purpose behind the schedule snafu. She smiled softly and whispered to Sherry, "I think it was to talk to you."

The missionary quoted something from the Bible, a verse that just happened to be the same passage Sherry had been meditating on for the past few weeks, and said she felt strongly that God was giving Sherry a message to learn more Scripture. They ended the conversation talking about the New Orleans marathon and the woman told Sherry to read 2 Timothy 1:7; not only is it one of her favorite verses, but she notices the number 217 everywhere. Right after Sherry gathered her belongings to get off the plane, the woman touched her arm and said, "One last thing. I think you need to run the race with your friend."

While my dear friend had no intention and I'm sure no desire to run the marathon, she decided to sign up at the very last minute. Sherry figured her rendezvous with this stranger was too coincidental to be mere happenstance. We both believed God was trying to tell or show us something.

The day we arrived, Sherry and I walked around the expo, a packed event where you can buy, look at, or sample hundreds of running products. Vendors lined row after row with colorful tables and bold banners, offering running apparel and gear, training products, food samples, anything you could possibly want to check out if running was your thing. But amidst the frenzy of exhibitions and the crowds that hungrily flocked to vendors that were giving out free sports drinks and energy bars, there was one booth that immediately caught my eye.

A bright banner blazed cheerily above an elderly gentleman who manned a table with a sign that read "Team 413." I was inexplicably drawn to the booth and couldn't help but strike up a conversation with the man in charge of the booth. I was curious to find out what "413" stood for.

Based on the Bible verse found in Philippians 4:13 which says, "I can do all things through Christ who gives me strength," Team 413 is a ministry created specifically for runners to fellowship with other athletes in the organization and to encourage them and others to run the race of life with truth, compassion, and boldness. I was inspired by the message and bought the book he was selling plus a couple of cool-looking T-shirts. Only after flipping through the book did I realize the old man was the one who started the ministry. I wore the 413 T-shirt the whole weekend. After experiencing a handful of God-ordained circumstances, how could I not?

Sherry and I had some time to kill before the race so we explored the city. I remembered sitting in the Traverse City airport when I first found out our flight was delayed. I had been bummed because I believed the delay would inevitably turn our New Orleans trip into a mad rush. We'd have time for nothing, I thought, except for me to run 26.2 miles, hopefully catch a catnap, and go home. But that wasn't the case; it seemed that once we got to the Big Easy, time stood still. We had plenty of time to take in the sights without scrambling to keep a tight schedule and stressing out because we ran five minutes late here or ten minutes late there.

Sherry and I were both unusually relaxed and calm and felt the presence of God with us every step of the way, reminding us of the blessings He gives even when our plans go awry. Practically every corner we turned, we caught a glimpse of a "God wink" in some form—from finding a coffee shop named PJ's, a nickname we affectionately call our pastor; to finding a limited edition New Orleans Starbucks mug to add to my massive collection; to being panicked because our hotel didn't have any coffee on race morning and though all the coffee shops in town were closed because of the big event, we stumbled into an open Starbucks in an unusually quiet and random section of town. It was like a "God winks" fest.

Sherry and I finished the race and we both felt great. She was ecstatic over her performance, considering she hadn't run in six months and did not train for this exhausting run. After we stretched for a bit, doused ourselves with water, chomped on some fruit and other snacks, we walked over to what seemed like a mile long line to climb aboard a bus that would take us back to the starting line.

Before we had to wait in line, one of the race volunteers approached us and said, "Hi ladies, we're opening a new line over there." She thumbed in the direction of an empty, line-free bus that just pulled up around the corner. "Go ahead and hop on." It was like someone was in front of us clearing the way. It wasn't just a fickle feeling, however; I believed it to be divine intervention. It was another sign that God was in back, in front, and on the side of us the entire trip, opening our eyes to His amazing works, however small, filling our hearts with gratitude, and showing us glimpses of His provision along the way. It was what Sherry and I both needed at the time. God knew what He was doing when He dropped her name into my mind the week before. He always does. It was a great race.

While I have had plenty of monumental races that forged in me a renewed spirit, there were others that were grueling. I think about the Paris marathon, the hardest race I ever ran. Running in European races is different than running in American ones. For starters, there's a language barrier. Also, at the time I ran, there were no water stations. I was used to drinking Gatorade or water every two miles. For some reason, Parisians didn't need to be hydrated, so I followed suit for six hours and ran without once quenching my thirst.

Did I forget to mention they also didn't think porta-potties were a necessity? Not only can the French physically exert themselves without the need for hydration, they also have no shame in dropping their pants and doing their business on the side of the road. Call me a prudish American, but I couldn't do it. I ran for six hours holding it in. But it wasn't all bad. I finished. I got a medal to add to my collection. And I learned that even though I was running in circumstances that were not the best, I could still accomplish my goal. Success isn't circumstantial; success is about attitude.

By the way, I recently visited New Orleans and bought a *fleur de lis* necklace, a French symbol representing simplicity and purity. It was a reminder of how life changing my trip with Sherry was and how I needed to keep my life pure and simple.

❦

You know what was so crazy? While I initially started running to get from Point A to Point B faster and to burn more calories, it didn't turn me into a beanpole, which I secretly hoped would happen. I felt like a freak show because I didn't look like the average runner. I didn't weigh a hundred pounds soaking wet and run around town and in marathons wearing a skimpy jogging bra and tiny spandex hot pants. I was an avid runner with more jiggling around than the common running folk. Sometimes it depressed me, although I had pride in my accomplishments. And trust me, I was proud of myself; running just one marathon is not as easy as it looks.

I had over-trained in 2008 and probably ran more races than I should have, so running started to be challenging. My body felt weak so I trained less. Training less meant I was less prepared for races. I also came to a point where I started rewarding myself with a little sweet here and a little treat there. My running ultimately became a defense mechanism instead of something I was doing to better myself.

I was associating running with food, which sucked the fun out of it and made it seem like a chore. It made me despise the moment I had to lace up my shoes and head out the door. My nerves were in the same kind of knotty bundle as if I were in a dentist's chair opening wide for the tortuous-sounding drill coming in for a root canal. So I took time off and stopped running.

Wouldn't you know it, after a few months passed from my well-needed break, I was aching to get back out on the road. I couldn't wait to pound the pavement with my new running shoes. And I was dying to sign up for some races.

Sometimes we put so much pressure on ourselves to do x, y, or z that we can corrupt those things with our fears and soil their beauty with our misaligned priorities, as I did with running. So we have to stop and get our intentions back in the right place. I learned this in therapy. I was so overwhelmed with my anxiety and my unquenchable appetite to please everyone and was crushed when I found out running—though without a doubt it paved a way for me to believe in myself—wasn't the miracle drug to transform me into a confident, skinny, and well-taken care of woman. I knew it was time to seek outside help.

I wish I had started therapy years ago but the truth is, I wasn't ready. I truly believe when we are at our wit's ends and we are finally ready to change, transformation happens. Step by step. Bit by bit. Through the process, peace can come in unusual ways.

Therapy didn't just change my approach to losing weight, it taught me a lot about myself. Some things that I didn't want to face.

7
Rethink the Shrink

"Be who you are and say what you feel, because those who mind
don't matter, and those who matter don't mind."

~ Dr. Seuss

"I'm lonely." I blurted out those two words while Dr. McDonald stared at me with compassion and handed me a box of Kleenex.

It was September of 2009 and I was at my new therapist's cushy office at the forceful advice of my nutritionist. I was there, I thought, for her to figure out what was wrong with me and fix it. Dr. McDonald was a weight counselor, but as I quickly found out, her main objective wasn't to play mechanic and give me a tune up. I wasn't paying her to look under my psychological hood and see what wires were short-circuited or check if my oil level was too low.

She was simply to be my guide in opening my eyes to certain truths I had been ignoring for too long—from realizing that God has a specific plan for my life, to discovering how to live in peace in a turbulent situation, to learning that I can't save the world, to realizing I had to take care of myself and in doing so, it was okay to put myself first sometimes.

I'll admit, I was pretty disappointed that Dr. McDonald wouldn't be telling me exactly how to do these things by offering me a step-by-step guide or cookie-cutter plan. I would do the work to figure it out for myself.

The initial session was overwhelming. I broke down. For the first time in a long time, I allowed the emotions that I had carefully sidelined to surface. On that particular appointment, my blubbering talk revolved around my sister's tragic death. I purged my grief without holding anything back. I even surprised myself by the amount and intensity of feelings that came out. I talked to her about my family dynamic and learned that my outburst wasn't so outrageously dramatic.

Although I was the youngest child in my family, I had to be the strong one. When Carol died, I had to pick myself up by the bootstraps and put on a resilient front, mainly for my parents. I didn't cry in front of them. I didn't cry around them. I kept my tears bottled up and tightly shut. It was safer that way. I thought that if my parents saw me upset, my behavior would reinforce their own sadness. I'd make them feel worse and why would I want to do that? I was the good daughter after all, the one who appeased them. I was the peacemaker who quickly and adeptly soothed any ripples on the otherwise clear and calm familial surface.

As I sat in Dr. McDonald's office, dabbing at my eyes and blowing my nose with crumpled tissues, I realized how much Carol had taught me and how much she even changed the path of my life. I can see now how she groomed me for the kind of life that I would end up living. If it weren't for my sister introducing me to the finer things in life and showing me that a better life existed, not just struggling, worrying, and forgetting about my own needs amidst the world of young children, I don't know how I would ever have been ready to fully embrace my path.

My sister also believed in Mike long before I ever did. I almost feel embarrassed for admitting that, but it's true. Carol and Mike had the same free-spirited and entrepreneurial fire. She tried to prepare me for my husband's success. Carol and Mike had an uncanny connection. They shared a passion for believing in and working toward their dreams.

These two special people in my life were dream chasers. Mike would share his vision of the future with my sister, and she'd excitedly take it in and encourage him to pursue whatever it was. Carol got him. She didn't think he was nuts or that his ideas were lofty or out of reach; she whole-heartedly respected his ambitions.

Therapy continued to bring to light other issues that had shadowed my life and contributed to me feeling anxious, lost, and without purpose. Money was one issue. I was living from a mentality of scarcity even when money wasn't short and I had more than enough. The fact was, I was fearful of letting go of every dollar. I'm thankful that my husband didn't share my mentality. Even when we were broke, Mike always believed that the proverbial pie was big enough. Whereas he lived his life believing everyone could have a slice of prosperity, blessing and success, I believed I'd have to fight tooth and nail for the last crumb.

I remember the first time I ever held a hundred dollar bill in my hand. During one of our financially challenging seasons, Mike and I went away somewhere for work and were given a wad of hundred dollar bills for the trip. I tucked one away in my wallet. It made me feel rich. I didn't want to spend it, not even on food, because I was afraid of letting it go. I remember feeling heartbroken when I had to use the bill on something I needed from the drug store. To look down and see an empty wallet was depressing.

I didn't realize a slip of paper could make me feel so

powerful. At the time, I was worried about paying the next utility bill and making sure we had food in our fridge. Letting go of the bill made me scared, like I'd never see that kind of money again. Spending that bill started my fear that we would not have enough financially.

I constantly played the what-if game. What if Mike doesn't get enough clients? What if this is our last big deal? What if we can't go to the next level? What if this project doesn't work out? My battle with the scarcity mentality makes me think of Edwene Gaine's book, *The Four Spiritual Laws of Prosperity*.

The author wrote this book with the foundation that we live in an abundant world where whatever we need or want can and will be provided for. She also shares how God is our source. Not our boss, not a thriving economy, not our fat bank account, not our wealthy grandparents, not our cushy retirement plan. God and God alone is who provides. So even in a world of financial turbulence or instability, we don't have to worry about what we need. If we trust Him, God will make a way.

These concepts were revolutionary to me. And challenging. They forced me to listen to the off-key music I had on repeat in my head, the tune that I had to hold on to and hoard whatever I could because I never knew what was going to happen in the future.

That fear played out in the oddest of places. When I traveled, I never unpacked my suitcase. I just opened it and left it unzipped, just in case I needed to leave early and go home. I could never enjoy being in the moment on vacations because I was inundated with thoughts of having to leave. When I went shopping with my first stylist, I bought two or three of the same items of clothing I liked the best, just in case one ripped or got dirty and couldn't be fixed or cleaned. I wanted to have a backup just in case. At one point, I even saved up $100,000 that I hid from Mike. I wanted to have a secret cushion just in case something went wrong, one of us got sick, he lost his job or we lost our money in, say, a devastating fire or flood. My financial philosophy revolved around "just in case."

Losing money wasn't the only thing that scared me. I was also afraid of losing Mike. I had a terrible time trying to communicate what I wanted from him, whether it was something simple like holding my hand or giving me a kiss when he came home from work. I didn't want to cause an unnecessary argument or discussion. Half the time, I didn't even know what I wanted in our relationship.

For instance, I simultaneously craved and refused physical intimacy. I wanted it, but I was afraid to have it. Instead of seeking closeness in Mike, I sought it in my children and even in my pets. Animals give unconditional love. They don't talk back. They don't want much. And they're pretty easy to take care of. Just feed them, make sure they have enough exercise, and show them some attention every now and then. I love cuddling up with my cats and dogs and sleeping with their warm bodies. They are always happy to see me and can sense when I'm sad.

It was a lot easier to lavish my attention on my pets than my husband because they doted on me whenever I needed it. It was hard for me to exert energy and affection to a man who was rarely at home and wrapped up in his world of success and vision.

I did the same thing with my kids. I focused on them instead of my marriage. They're growing up so fast and itching for the chance to spread their wings. It makes me want to hold on to them with everything in me. On one hand, I'm thrilled that they're becoming independent and making their own steps in this world; on the other hand, it reminds me that soon they will leave the nest. It makes me sad and also makes me think about the distance that has grown between Mike and me. Distance that I did nothing to keep from growing.

When I started therapy, I learned I needed to speak my piece to my husband. The roles needed to be reversed. After years of me supporting, encouraging and sacrificing so he could live out his dreams, I needed my husband to turn his attention my way. I certainly wasn't going to go cold turkey and stop supporting, encouraging, and sacrificing for him, but I needed things from him, things he probably couldn't have given me because he had no clue I needed them. How is any man supposed to know what we need from them if we are tight-lipped?

I used to hold in my feelings and opinions; I'm more open about them now with my husband. Of course, this is a big change for Mike. He's not used to having me express myself emotionally, especially if I feel strongly about something or even angry. I know there is a balance with communication. I can't just spew venom because I feel like it or because I just "feel" it. I am working on relaying my thoughts in a way that is not defensive or cutthroat, but effective. Believe me, it's a hard balance for me to find and maintain, but I know our relation-ship is stronger for it.

❧

When I started working on this book, my dad and I had many long talks about my childhood. The topic of our conver-sations repeatedly reverted to my mother and her issues with depression. I've realized through talking with my father that the issues I faced when I finally decided to get therapy were rooted in my mother's mental illness.

My dad shared how when I was three years old, my

mom would call him at work and tell him, "I'm taking off." She'd make her announcement with a relentless defiance and would be gone for a couple of hours. I really believe all my mom needed was a break. My dad would come home to an empty house not knowing where she had gone. While I don't remember these frequent temporary exits, Dr. McDonald made me ask myself if my deep-rooted fear of abandonment had anything to do with her antics. Probably.

Working through my internal struggles wasn't just about my mother or about me dealing with the repercussions of her illness. It was also about seeing traces of that depression in Sara. Do you know what it feels like to walk into your daughter's room and see her sobbing uncontrollably on the bed, crying about how lonely, unhappy, and miserable she is? The pain ripped through my heart, a pain similar to what I felt when my mother cried and I was unable to fix her sadness.

I don't want my daughter to have to go through life feeling lonely and anxious. Sara deserves more than that. While I have tempered my anxiety through better self-care and therapy, I am also aware of how I can empower her when her mental battles cripple her. I can be the example. I can show her the ropes. I can teach her because I am doing it myself.

As I'm learning to live by the philosophy of letting go—letting go of anger, unforgiveness, insecurities, fears, and control—my anxiety has dwindled to intermittent whispers instead of incessant screaming. I've also let go of my all-or-nothing attitude. If things don't go my way, the world isn't going to end. And if I can't fix every problem or make everyone happy, you know what happens? My life still goes on. I refuse to drown in worry because life isn't as perfect as I would like it to be. I know if I can make such strides, my daughter can too.

⊘⃛

The general anxiety I suffered had far-reaching effects including my weight. I lived for diets. I spent so much time on diets it was like a full-time job. It was ironic; anxiety, the main culprit in my battle of the bulge, was what catapulted me to visit Dr. McDonald.

Right before I started therapy, I went on a 21-day weight challenge. For three weeks, I restricted my calories and bullied my body into following a strict eating regime, consuming nothing but a green, slimy drink at specific times during the day. It was hard, but it was only for 21 days. I figured I could do anything for 21 days, even drink sludge.

When I found out that this special diet wasn't just limited to the three-week induction period, and that I'd have to drink the nauseating magic potion for the rest of my life if I wanted to see lasting results, I balked. It was ridiculous. And totally unbalanced. It wasn't how I wanted to lose weight. Even seeing some fat melt off didn't encourage me enough to want to live the rest of my life in a diet coop. I didn't want to have to give up a little something sweet or salty once in a while. We can't all be health Nazi's a hundred percent of the time. Isn't moderation key?

So although I initially dove into the program with reckless abandon, I quickly became frustrated. Although my clothes felt looser after a few days, the weight loss suddenly stopped. It seemed I was eating less and exercising more, but instead of continually losing, I was gaining weight. The equation didn't make any sense. I couldn't figure out where I was going wrong.

I headed to my nutritionist armed with a bulging file folder full of results from blood tests, allergy tests, a body composition analysis, and other medical reports that proved nothing was physically wrong with me. I wanted to show her the evidence that I wasn't being 'bad' and indulging poor diet behaviors. On the contrary, I was being 'good', but my weight loss was still at a standstill.

My nutritionist took a look at the folder and blankly told me, "See a therapist, Becky. I bet your anxiety is what's keeping you from losing weight." And wouldn't you know it, she was right. Being in therapy made me look in the mirror and confront the habits I had unconsciously formed that (surprise! surprise!) were undermining my health efforts.

I assumed I was putting in the work of a diet champion, but in many ways I was aborting my own success. Starving myself and being a masochist when I ate something bad were not ingredients to living a healthy lifestyle. Who knows? You might relate to my behaviors.

I refused to forgive myself if I had a bite (or two or five) of something I was not supposed to eat. If I ate a spoonful of lasagna, a scoop of chocolate ice cream, or the sliver of pizza leftover from one of my kid's dinner plates, you'd think I had committed a crime. I thought that spoonful, scoop, or sliver would be the death of me. I imagined it would make the number on the scale five times higher than it had been hours earlier.

Those extra indulgences haunted me with their scathing words, "See, Becky? You have no willpower. You are out of control. You'll never be thin. You'll never be happy." Then I would have to make reparations for the damage I did to my body. I would run. But not a quick run. Why run only three miles? If I was going to get dressed and head out on the road or hop on a treadmill, I should run for at least five or six miles. Why waste the energy if I was only going to be working out for thirty minutes? There was no point. I had an all-or-nothing attitude—don't eat and do exercise a lot. If I eat too much, exercise more and, of course, be disgusted with and berate myself in the process. And during or after I beat myself up, maybe have a snack. Or two. You know, to soothe myself.

I lived by the scale. I weighed myself two, three, four times a day. And whenever I'd look down at the number, whatever it was, it never made me happy. Just more agitated. I hated myself because I lacked self-control. I couldn't help having the extra bites of food. I couldn't help not eating perfectly outside of my severely restrictive diets. At the same time, I was also tired. I was tired of cooking one meal for the family and a separate, healthier version for me. It was almost easier to give up and do nothing. If I didn't try, I didn't have to worry about failure. Then again, I wouldn't have to think about succeeding either.

Therapy revealed how I could never be happy trying to lose weight this way. It didn't work in the past and it would never work in the future. Why? Because diets are quick fixes. Easy outs. A short-term solution to a long-term problem. The underlying issue needs to be dealt with before you can take care of your mind, body, and soul in a healthy way. My anxiety and my obsession over food, diets, and exercise prevented me from experiencing permanent weight loss. It was time to stop.

What works for you might be different and that's okay, but I noticed a huge difference in my health and well-being when I started eating intuitively. I needed to retrain myself to eat only when I was hungry and stop when I was full. Doesn't it sound so easy? Anyone can do it, right? Don't be fooled. Once you start eating that way, you quickly find out how hard it really is.

I was used to eating whenever I was stressed or upset or sad or frustrated. And I didn't have a gauge in my system that would warn me when my belly had had enough. I just kept going and going and going until I got to the point where I was almost sick, I ate too much. By then, it was too late. The damage was done. I'd cycle back to hating myself and running extra miles to compensate for my screw-up.

I'm getting better. Dr. McDonald has been instrumental in helping me balance my health the right way by teaching me how to eat better and intuitively and to really listen to my body. I don't have to deny an occasional treat. She has also reintroduced to me the joys of exercising, not as a means of compensating for something unhealthy I ate, but to take pleasure in the physical movement and how my body feels alive and empowered.

As time goes by, I can see how learning to eat intuitively has helped me gracefully rest at a natural weight. While the battle with my pounds is an ongoing struggle, I'm definitely not as hard on myself about it as I used to be. Instead, I nurture myself in a positive way. Without Dr. McDonald, I'd probably be back in the vicious cycle.

❦

Perhaps the hardest topic I had to comb through in therapy was my sense of purpose or lack thereof.

Mathematician and meteorologist Edward Lorenz came up with a theory that scientists initially thought was ludicrous but now it's widely accepted. It's called the Butterfly Effect. Lorenz believed that a butterfly's wings are able to create a small change in the atmosphere that can ultimately set off a chain of events that could affect the creation of a major storm or natural disaster, kind of like a domino effect. Though the flapping of their wings don't necessarily cause, let's say, a tornado, the movement does offer a profound impact on whether or not the storm comes into being.

Through therapy I have found that my responsibility is not to save or change the world, but simply to flap here and there. When I do, its effect will be felt somewhere, somehow.

This principle goes against my nature. I want to pay it forward in monumental ways. I want to end homelessness, hunger, and save kids from abuse of any kind. I want to end suffering and anguish. I want to live the Miss Universe dream of bringing peace to the world. But earth to Becky, I cannot.

My son Taylor came home from school one day with an assignment. He was told to write down what he wanted to do with his life. "Mom, this is so stupid," he said. Then he posed the question to me, "What do you want to do?"

I thought for a moment and answered, "I want to be a philanthropist, of course."

"What's that?"

"Doing nice things for other people. That's what I want to do."

It's true. I do for people when I can and what I can. But the pressure is finally off for me to shoulder the world's burdens—or even the burdens in my community—to solve every little or big problem. Most of the time, it's not about making changes on a grand scale; it's about doing the little things. Flapping your wings may not seem like a big deal, but it is.

Recently, I bought two pieces of the Miss Universe crown. The original crown was made up of 553.64 grams of 14k gold, 18k gold, and platinum. It was jeweled in such an elaborate and stunning way; it was too heavy for the winner to wear. So the arches over the top of the crown were removed and reworked to create what is called a Fair Maiden pendant.

The pendant is stunning. It has a 2.46 carat pear-shaped lab-created ruby in the middle; the ruby is surrounded by a swirl of diamond simulated accents in the shape of the Miss Universe sash. When I saw it for the first time, it reminded me that although I can't create a happy and safe world, I can flap my wings like the butterfly to make a change in that direction.

I wanted four pendants, one for me and one for each of my daughters, but I could only get two as only 200 were sold. I gave one to Sara who put it on a beautiful chain and I'm saving the other one for Morgan until she is old enough to appreciate and wear it. No, I didn't leave Madison out. I got her something special as well.

I've always looked at my purpose in life like it was something that was concrete. Like an in-depth calculated outline of what exactly I was supposed to do. It's probably because my husband was so sure of his dreams and what he was meant to do. There was no questioning. No floundering. No looking in this direction or that direction for a sign or for guidance. But I wasn't my husband. And no matter how much I secretly hoped that his dreams would overflow and spill over into my life, I had to create my own path.

Creating my own butterfly effect was part of that path. Before I could even begin to determine what God wanted me to do in my life, I had to start living like it was the small things that matter. Like being kind to my neighbor. Like carrying the groceries for the elderly woman in the store. Like spending time talking to someone who is feeling down. Like being present with my children without obsessing over my random anxious and racing thoughts. Like acting a little nicer during the holidays instead of stressing about gift-giving, not finding a parking spot at the mall, or standing in long lines. And sometimes it means giving financially to someone in need if you are blessed to have the ability to do that. I strongly believe we can all give somewhere, no matter what our income is or how much we have in our wallets. See? Little flaps. Big difference.

I used to be on edge trying to figure out what my unique path was on this earth until my therapist helped me see that it was okay if I didn't know what that was just yet. It was okay if I didn't have a specific dream or vision or objective or goal in mind. It was okay not to be the architect of a grand plan to change the world. It was okay, she even said, if I felt a little lost at times.

The Bible says that we are like sheep. We've all gotten lost and have gone astray. There are days I feel like a lost bull in a china shop, causing catastrophe and chaos wherever I go, but I've come to accept that thought as a mere state of mind. It's not true; it's simply a thought that I alone have the power to believe or disbelieve. I create my lost feeling because I don't know how to respond to things in a positive way.

The truth is, I'm not lost. I'm still fluttering about making small changes here and small changes there that I am confident will create a climactic effect. What those changes are I haven't a clue. I don't even think it matters. It just matters that I'm trying and putting one foot in front of the other and living out this theory.

Flapping my wings doesn't mean I'm perfect and I do the right thing all the time; it just means I can make the choice to quiet my anxious thoughts, stop participating in what-if games, and keep on believing that life offers all of us a huge pie that never decreases in size because there is always more than enough for you and for me.

I do believe that everyone is put on this earth for a specific reason. We make the choice whether or not to act on that innate calling, but if we take the risk I believe we can live a life that reaches beyond our wildest dreams. My vision for my life is getting a whole lot clearer. The closer I get to what I'm supposed to do, the more I find the unadulterated and indescribable happiness I had when I was a little girl, when I was oblivious to hardship, trials, fears, or worry. But it's even better than that. It's not a feeling of naïveté; it's one of freedom, of ease, and most importantly one of peace. My time is coming. I can feel it.

All these eye-opening epiphanies helped me forge my path of change. I think the biggest lesson I learned is that I can't amend what happened in the past. True, I am shaped today based on the events of my past. We all are. We are living a blueprint created from how we were raised, what happened to us as a child, how our parents treated us, how we learned to deal with money, love, and circumstances, and how we received positive or negative influences along our life journey.

But if we're living a crummy life, we can change the architecture of our blueprint going forward. We can't erase the traumatic memories of being abused, for instance, but we can choose how to live from a place of inner health and healing. We can't erase the bad financial decisions we made, but we can choose to make better ones going forward. We can't erase the mistakes we made that may have ended our marriage, but we can choose not to repeat those mistakes and work on developing ourselves so we can give our best to others.

Change is never easy. Especially positive change. I think it's easier to be negative and live life as a worry-wart, a Debbie-the-Downer, or Pity-Party Patty. It's definitely more challenging to stand up in the face of trials, depression, and obstacles and live a life of meaning or purpose. It takes time and energy. It takes reading empowering books. It takes learning. It can even take some therapy appointments to sift through pieces of the past that led to you being unhappy.

That's what I had to do. I had to uncover why I was so miserable, and that discovery made me desperate to continue making changes. I don't think I realized how hard or how long it would take. I hoped it would be instantaneous. Like a microwave delivery from my old way of thinking, being, and acting. No such luck. The peace and contentment I wanted required some hard work and time for me to get it.

Did you know that during takeoff a plane uses about half

of its fuel? Once it's in the air and flying to its destination, it doesn't need as much. When we decide to change a part of our lives for the better—to get healthy, to have peace, to find forgiveness, to search for healing, to stop an addiction—the genesis of getting started is when the most work is needed, when you take the initial stand and say, "I know I have to change and I want to make a change."

Therapy wasn't a cure-all and certainly didn't fix all my problems. It's why I'm still committed to seeing a therapist when I need to talk through some issues. Time creates lasting change. I cannot repeat that enough. Even after I was making some heavy-duty change, there was a lot more muck I needed to dig up and walk through.

I've found that when you start working on transforming your life, random holes start to pop up out of nowhere. Just when you think an a-ha! moment has permanently changed your life, and maybe it has, another area that needs some improvement shows up. It's kind of annoying. Like cleaning your house from top to bottom and realizing there are more cobwebs in the corner and dust balls under the bed and hidden laundry in your children's closets. But as annoying as it is, you know the work needs to be done.

8
Searching for My Inner Vixen

"A girl should be two things: classy and fabulous."
- COCO CHANEL

———————◆———————

*M*ike grabbed me by the hand and led me to the front row. The front row of the 500 plus people-filled auditorium. The front row of the room packed with beautiful women who donned dress slacks, chic blouses, and tailored blazers. The front row where I'd stick out like a sore thumb in jeans, a sweatshirt, and running shoes. I was mortified but Mike didn't notice my unease. He had already planted himself on a chair and whipped out his trusty notebook and pen, anxious to hear what the brilliant entrepreneurial sensation Ali Brown had to say and ready to jot down every spoken word.

My husband couldn't tell how uncomfortable I was because he was overwhelmed with the excitement of the conference. Mike eagerly scooted up to the edge of his seat and scanned the stage which was draped in a burgundy velvet curtain. His eyes darted left and right anticipating the moment when Ali would step out in a creative and mind-blowing grand entrance to mark the start of the event.

Mike wasn't the only one rapt with a pre-conference high. The auditorium echoed with the chatter and laughter of energized entrepreneurs and idea generators, most of whom were women, who were pumped up to learn how to create or grow their business and how to turn their idea into a money-making dream come true. I didn't pay attention to the talk from these ladies about what business they had started or what new client they locked in or what they wanted to get out of Ali's event. I did, however, pay attention to the shoes.

Glossy high heels. Chunky boots. Stiletto peep toes. Fur-lined booties. Sparkly ballerina flats. Strappy pumps. I looked down at my feet and was greeted by my worn Asics. I remembered Mike's words as we were packing for the weekend conference trip to Las Vegas. "What do I bring?" I asked as my eyes landed on my empty suitcase which looked quite lonely next to his stuffed carry-on bag. "It's casual so casual stuff, I guess," my husband replied as he tried to jam another pair of socks into one of the already bulging compartments.

Casual. Casual means comfortable. Like lounging around the house comfortable, right? So I packed casual. I packed jeans and my favorite and most comfortable sweat outfits and figured my running shoes would do the trick for the next few days. Nobody told me casual meant business casual. A little under Sunday best casual. Or more importantly, not jeans and sweatshirt casual.

When the conference began, I noticed cameramen positioned around the room videotaping the audience from every angle. When one would sweep my way, I'd look down, steer my head in the opposite direction, or bend toward the ground pretending to reach for something in my purse. I did whatever I could do to make sure I was not recorded. God forbid anyone should notice my careless-looking outfit.

As different speakers began to address the audience and

offer timeless insights into the world of entrepreneurship, Mike was assiduously scribbling down notes. I mirrored his furious jotting, except I wasn't writing down ideas or nuggets of wisdom the wonderful speakers shared. I was writing that I needed a change. That I needed to start feeling better about myself. That I needed to find out what I was going to do with my life. That I needed to once and for all get out of this rut. That I needed to start taking care of myself.

During the break, I looked around the room and watched the hundreds of women who mingled around with self-assured posture and beaming smiles. You know what amazed me? It wasn't that they wore dressy clothes or looked like supermodels. It was much more than that. They were all unique. They were of different shapes and sizes. Big. Small. Curvy. Lean. Muscular. Voluptuous. They all had one thing in common—they were confident and that's what made them beautiful.

I knew at that moment I was ready to take the plunge and step out of my comfort zone. I had to stop neglecting my appearance. And yes, it was time to trash the sweats. That night I lay in bed in a beautiful hotel room at the Palazzo and the image of my comfy, cotton, elastic-banded jogging pants kept flashing before my eyes. *They had to go*, I thought. *The affair was over*.

Unlike me, these ladies didn't cover up their bodies in big and baggy clothes. Their style was fitted. Fitted and fashionable. They were ready to unveil themselves to the world in all their glory. I wanted that same unwavering boldness. I didn't want to change who I was, I just wanted to resurrect and unleash her into this world. I wanted to let the real me out of the hole I had buried myself in.

It was the perfect time, having just started therapy and already feeling the flickers of change rumble in my belly. I had even taken a baby step. I was starting to do small things for myself to give evidence to my desire to take care of myself. The day before the event, I bought myself a beautiful pair of shoes that cost just under a thousand dollars. Not that I could really wear them. They were too fancy to match the loads of sweatshirts and jeans I had packed.

When I arrived in Las Vegas for the Ali Brown conference, I was excited because I love Sin City. I always have a good time there. Partly because it's an ideal spot to people-watch and partly because there is so much commotion and hoopla and lights and shows and craziness going on, that people don't really pay any attention to you. It's an easy place to fit in because everyone else is concerned with having a good time, not what you look like or what you're wearing. I'm also very comfortable in Vegas because Carol had been taking me there on luxury excursions for a long time. I knew my way around the Strip as well as any local.

There I was walking around the main drag, feeling like a sardine in the middle of throngs of people crowding the sidewalk "ooohing" and "ahhing" their way down the street. In a circus of a hundred different languages, tourists were gaping at the stunning display of architecture from the replica of the Eiffel Tower to the majestic stance of Caesars Palace to the dancing Bellagio Fountains. As many times as I've been to Vegas, I admit, I still get a little awestruck from time to time.

None of the wonder, however, could keep my mind off a painful blister pulsing on my foot. Why is it that the smallest thing can sometimes be the biggest pest? My shoes, the ones I had worn on the plane that I thought were hip and chic enough for Vegas, were too small and dug into the heel of my right foot creating and aggravating a major pus-filled blister. I was also walking in a half-marathon the following weekend, so I couldn't afford to have any unnecessary injuries prevent me from finishing the race.

It was time to get new shoes. New shoes that would likely cost me a lot of dough. I don't know if you've ever been shopping in Las Vegas, but the stores are a little different than what a typical suburban neighborhood offers. You're not going to find a Payless, TJ Maxx, or Target anywhere on the strip or in the malls. And you're not going to pay less than $200 for a pair of shoes, except maybe for a pair of flimsy flip-flops, but that's not the point.

I walked into Salvatore Ferragamo. My sister once told me they made fabulous shoes. I had never bought any before or even tried on a pair, but I took Carol's word to heart. She was the fashion guru after all. When I walked into the boutique, I felt a bit out of my element. Brightly lit with gold furnishings and a gleaming white marble floor mirroring the reflection of the entire room, the shop radiated opulence and an untouchable glamour. Only a handful of shoes were displayed on top of miniature glass cases that were strategically placed around the room to give off a classic, uncluttered appearance.

Two tall, beanpole-shaped women wearing tight black outfits and blank expressions on their chiseled European faces acknowledged my presence with a nod. One voiced a breathy, "Good morning."

I headed straight for the sales rack positioned in the corner of the back of the store and smirked when I saw the display. The discounted footwear wasn't as neat and orderly as the regularly priced shoes. They were piled together almost like an afterthought, like a fairytale stepchild. I immediately feasted my eyes on a pair of black ankle booties. The leather was supple, buttery. The heel was just the right size. Not too small, not too high. The stitching was immaculate and when I tried them on, I felt like Cinderella finding the perfect shoe.

As always, Carol was right on.

I walked up to the cash register and started digging around my wallet for my credit card. I didn't know how much the shoes cost but figured since they were on sale they couldn't be that much. The woman behind the counter looked at me and smiled. With a heavy Russian accent she said, "Great choice. That will be $950."

I was a millisecond away from dropping my open wallet on the floor. *What?! And that was the sale price?* Though neon dollar signs were blazing in my mind, I remained calm and slapped my card on the counter. I acted as if, "Well, of course these booties are just under a thousand bucks. I'm actually thrilled because I thought they'd be more. I always spend as much money on a pair of shoes as people spend on their mortgage." What I was really thinking, however, was a more colorful version of "Holy crap!"

As I walked out of the store with my glossy black bag in tow, I couldn't help feeling stunned. I had to tell someone. I had just bought a fabulous pair of shoes that were beautiful and would last a lifetime, but I had never spent so much money on a small purchase like that in my life. It felt strange. Don't get me wrong. I loved the shoes; they were beautiful. But I felt guilty. Buyer's remorse was nipping at my heel, scraping at my blister.

How could I spend that much money when people are starving all over the world and even right here in Vegas? How could I spend so much when people are losing their jobs left and right? How could I spend so much when nations are at war, when the economy is floundering, when so many folks don't even have money to buy health insurance? It seemed like a frivolous expense.

I immediately texted my daughter and told her about my outrageous purchase. "Good for you," she replied. *Good for me.*

Maybe, but that's not how I felt. I didn't know how to enjoy my purchase without feeling guilty about it. But wait a minute. It wasn't like I spent exorbitant amounts of cash on stuff all the time, and even if I did, wasn't that still my prerogative? Why couldn't I benefit from some of the fruits of how hard my husband and I had worked all these years? We were finally able to enjoy a time sans frivolous lawsuits. Sans employees stealing money from us. Sans outstanding bills.

So why the persistent guilt? I know it stemmed from feeling I didn't deserve to make that transaction, a feeling of unworthiness that had pretty much ruled most of my life. That's probably why I didn't do a great job keeping up my appearance or caring for myself. I didn't think I deserved spending any kind of money on me.

This wasn't always the case. When I got married, I loved shopping, dressing up and wearing a suit to work, even if it was out on the ball field at the local park (I worked for a city parks and recreation department, so I had some meetings in outdoor venues). Over the years, I stopped paying attention to the reflection in the mirror. It was a combination of my growing waistline and lack of time. So I chose a wardrobe that was convenient and one I didn't have to think about.

Sweat pants became my friend. Jeans were the enemy because the dreaded muffin top never failed to make its uncomely appearance, and pants were just uncomfortable. As the years wore on, I noticed I had a closet full of sweat suits in a rainbow of colors. You name the color; I'd have an ensemble to match. I even had some dressy ones. Okay, "dressy" is probably an oxymoron for sweats, but there are some nice ones out there that are glittery and sparkly and have cool designs. Seriously.

It was safe to say I had lost my style over the years, so buying those Ferragamo shoes represented growth. It's funny.

The booties are collecting dust in my closet. They are officially eye candy because they don't fit well anymore. (Confession time: they never did fit properly. I squeezed my feet in them because they were all the rage...and on sale).

Give them away or donate them, you say? Never. I am far from stingy, but I just can't let them go because they have a lot to say. They tell me with pride that they were my first indulgence. They remind me to lay aside guilt and enjoy the little things in life, whether it's taking a bubble bath, getting a pedicure, talking a long walk, or buying a hot pair of shoes. And they bring me back to Vegas, the place where my sister and I gallivanted in the lap of luxury and the place where I took a leap from finally realizing I needed to change to taking an actual step in that direction.

The Ali Brown conference was slowly taking me to another level. I met people there who would influence me in ways I didn't fully appreciate until just recently. While the majority of these women were successful in their businesses and discovering new ways to expand and grow, I had just sold my business and wasn't sure what to do. When lunchtime rolled around, I had the option of sitting with attendees from the conference, total strangers mind you, and talking about business ideas. I also had the option to sneak away on my own to one of the many grand buffets that were beckoning my name. I chose to sneak away, but my stealth plan backfired.

My tattletale husband told Lisa Sasevich of my plans and that I'd be by myself during the break. Lisa was in Mike's mastermind group and I had met her a couple of times. I admired her. She was genuinely happy all of the time and had a great marriage.

Lisa made it her mission to hunt me down and drag me to lunch with her and a group of other women. At the time, I was ready to throw a tantrum and scream at the top of my lungs, "I just want to be alone!" But I was surprisingly gracious and accepted her offer.

Six women, sipping on sparkling water and munching on soft, doughy rolls with a melt-in-your-mouth buttery crust, rounded out a large table. Introductions were made that included your name and the dreaded what-you-do statement. I don't know what happened, but when my turn rolled around, the floodgates opened. I started crying as twelve eyes focused in on me like a giant laser beam. What was I going to say? "Hi, I'm Becky and I'm lost?" "Hi, I'm Becky and I'm a mom who wears sweatpants all day?" "Hi, I'm Becky and I still haven't figured out what I want to do?" In a tangled, knotted string of vowels and consonants that poured out of my blubbering mess, that's pretty much what I said.

Between the sobs, sniffles and snot, I joked about how I wanted to write a book about being married to a millionaire and going to therapy because of it. I wasn't even serious; I was just showing my sarcastic attitude. You know what happened? Lisa hopped on that bandwagon and took the reigns, encouraging mc in what I thought was a silly goal. "That's it," she exclaimed, practically rocketing out of her seat. She later told me she got chills when I mentioned it.

Lisa's words meant a lot to me and made me mull over the possibility that there was more out there, that maybe my ideas or the fluttering in my heart were indicators that I could do something with my life that was meaningful.

Something stirred inside me. At the time I wasn't ready to do something drastic like actually put my thoughts down on paper, but I was ready to keep treading down the road toward transformation. My therapist was bringing to light some internal issues I had to deal with and it was time to reinvent myself on the outside. Goodbye tennis shoes and sweats. Hello....um....okay, wasn't so sure yet, but hello something better.

☙

Before I could embark as a whole and peace-filled woman, there was the matter of evaluating what was going on with me on the outside. If I was reflecting my inner self in what I wore or how I looked, I was doing a poor job. But I didn't know. I was doing the best I could. With a husband, five children, a household and outside businesses to manage, taking care of myself on the outside was not my priority.

Truly, I know that appearance does matter. Not that we have to look like a supermodel, but we need to take pride in how we present ourselves. This looks different for everyone. For me it meant slapping on some makeup to brighten up my tired face. Throwing on lacey underwear instead of granny panties from my maternity days. Getting out of frumpy clothes and into something more edgy. Adorning myself with a pretty necklace instead of thinking my kid's dirty handprints on my T-shirt was an artistic accessory.

That's when I hired Shari, my first stylist. While she was great in pushing me out of my comfort zone and teaching me how to flatter my complexion and figure, there were a few glitches that popped up. And they ended up costing me tens of thousands of dollars and drawers and a closet full of couture clothing I never even wore. That's a hefty price to pay to learn something.

I woke up one morning and heard my daughter singing the song "Just the Way You Are" by Bruno Mars. It's now my theme song, but when I first heard the tune, it broke my heart.

The music was catchy and I found myself humming along, but I quickly stopped concentrating on the melody and started listening to the words. "When I see your face/There's not a thing that I would change/Cause you're amazing/Just the way you are."

The words were touching, and hearing my teenage daughter sing such affirming lyrics melted my heart. But I couldn't relate. I didn't find a connection with the song. I'm amazing just the way I am? I'm beautiful just like this? Really? Nope. I didn't believe it. If I was really beautiful, I thought, I wouldn't have to cover myself up all the time. I could just be me. But for some reason that still wasn't enough.

While I deserved kudos for crawling out of my style rut, there was still a disconnect. The beautiful clothes recommended to me weren't just more glamorous and colorful. I noticed they served a specific purpose, to hide my curves. I was told to wear pants that made my legs look slimmer, particular length of sleeves so attention wouldn't be drawn to my arms, and certain patterns to achieve a vertical effect. My fashion mantra seemed to be, "Cover up. Hide. Camouflage. Cover up more."

Wasn't that the opposite of what I needed to do? Wasn't I trying to come out of the proverbial closet? Wasn't I supposed to be emerging? What was the point of covering up? To mask a few trouble spots or pretend my voluptuousness didn't exist? Was I supposed to wear outfits on the grandma side to prove I was humble or modest? Honestly, I found it a bit stifling. I wanted to bust out of the iron prison and unveil my true inner sexiness that was finally dying to come out.

Deep down I knew God thought I was beautiful, but for once in my life I wanted to believe it for myself. I wanted to look in the mirror, stare into my own eyes, say out loud how beautiful I am, and nod with pride in that truth. But this new style I was adopting wasn't my channel to get there. Sure, I had changed my outside appearance, but the change wouldn't be complete without meshing it with inner change.

And now I had another problem—too much stuff. Since I had not fully worked on capturing and nurturing the inner me, the edgy me, I had developed compulsive shopping habits. Among other things, I had become a shoe fanatic. I think most women are. I remember standing in my closet one day and staring at over fifty pair of shoes, realizing that every two or three pair looked almost identical. I had bought shoes like people buy their morning lattes. Religiously. Frankly, it had become an obsession.

I loved shoes because I could fully express myself in the footwear of my choice. I could be wild. Vibrant. Sassy. Risqué. Seductive. I spent many waking hours and thousands of dollars buying shoes. One of the first things I wanted to do when I woke up each morning was check the handful of shoe websites I subscribed to. What was on sale? What styles were all the rage?

I became buddies with the store managers at Nordstrom's and quickly became their favorite customer. They'd call and email me whenever a new shipment of shoes would come in. They had my credit card on file and would charge the shoes they'd recommend to my account. They even opened up the store early just for me so I could shop in private. I felt like Julia Roberts in *Pretty Woman* being waited on hand and foot in the fancy boutique. The truth was, I loved being the center of attention. I loved having people show me favor. I loved getting special treatment. But I didn't love the fact that those warm and fuzzy feelings disappeared only hours later.

My compulsive behavior didn't stop there. Shoes weren't the only things I bought. My obsession had cousins. My handbag addiction was out of control. I couldn't buy just any handbag. I looked for the few seen on fashion runways, the one-of-a-kind bags that only adorned the thin arms of A-list celebrities and supermodels.

I also became a makeup junkie. Forget about heroin. Give me high shine lipsticks, glossy compacts with shimmery foundation, and eyeliner pencils in all the colors of the rainbow. I was anal about my makeup items. I took special care of them, even the drugstore kinds, and was careful not to scratch the cases.

But I was lucky. It's not like I was breaking the bank. I could wake up and afford to spend $7,000 on clothes, jewelry, bags, or makeup. It's not like I was causing our family to go into debt. And I wasn't doing anything harmful. I wasn't selling drugs or shoplifting or having affairs. I wasn't stealing from poor people or being mean to old folks or making fun of babies. I was spending money on stuff.

All the retail therapy in the world couldn't cure my problem. I hid behind sweatpants, then hid behind fancy designer clothes, then hid behind compulsive behavior, secretly hoping all these things would force the real me out of my shell. I was working backwards. Instead of taking care of my inside to find the real me, I was taking care of my outside to create a faux version. It wasn't working.

No amount of shoes, purses, or makeup would be enough to sift through and get rid of the pains, the feelings of unworthiness, and the overwhelming guilt. Nothing was enough because I had struggled my entire life with thinking I wasn't thin enough, pretty enough, or smart enough. I hoped material things would fill some of that lack, but they didn't. They just made me made feel worse.

I didn't feel like I was enough because I didn't even know who I was. I had a stylist who was trying to create a new identity for me that was the antithesis of who I really was. Instead of asking myself, "What do I want to project?" or "How do I want to express Becky Reese?" I kept relying on the opinions of others to figure it out for me. I ignored my question behind my compulsive shopping sprees.

I think part of my dilemma circled back to caring about what others thought about me and not wanting to rock the boat. I wasn't sure what people would think of my new self. Would they perceive me as too wild? Too sexy? Too bold? Too outrageous? Too much? Would they be uncomfortable with my new change? I didn't want to make anyone mad or disappointed by my transformation, so I went with the flow without interjecting my own spirit in the process. I mean really, let's say I had voiced some of my concerns to my first stylist, what could she possibly have done? Yelled at me? Thrown a cashmere pashmina in my face? Called me a hussy because I didn't mind baring just the slightest amount of cleavage?

I was starting to piss myself off. I snapped one day in therapy and admitted I'd had enough. Enough of allowing my choices to be influenced by the opinions and thoughts of others. Enough of not saying exactly how I felt or asking for what I wanted. Enough of feeling insecure and not standing up for myself.

That's when I met Tamara Gold, my current coach who has helped me make lasting change in so many areas. The first time my husband mentioned her name, I thought, "No way. She's too famous." Tamara works with the rich and famous, celebrities, soap opera stars, and award-winning musicians. What on earth would she do with a small town girl like me? I felt I had to be a pity case for me to get on her client roster. A year went by after that conversation with Mike and I forgot all about it.

Then one day, out of the clear blue, I decided to check out her website again and filled out an online report. A few weeks later at an Ali Brown event, I saw her sitting behind us and Mike kept nudging me to say hello. I was shy in my introduction, but she certainly wasn't. Tamara grabbed my hands and pulled them close to her face. Before I continue, you need to know that I have a problem with people touching me. It freaks me out. I like to keep pretty big personal boundaries between me and other people. So when Tamara reached out for my hands, I was startled. But to my surprise I didn't feel awkward or uncomfortable or annoyed. Instead I was immediately captured by her mesmerizing spell.

My heart was beating a mile a minute as she told me how beautiful I was. I tried with all my strength not to let the tears that were forming fall down my face and ruin whatever makeup I had on. I blurted out how I thought she was too good to work with me, not a confident and witty introduction. The rest of our conversation is a blur. I just knew at that moment I had found the person to work with me.

The first thing Tamara did when we started was give me a workbook. In it were pages and pages of homework assignments, all writing projects having to do with delving into myself and finding my identity. I wrote about my fears. About my wants. About my desires. About my insecurities. She knew in order to bring out my style, she had to bring out me.

There's more. Tamara made me start each morning and end each night by writing down five things I was grateful for. Wow, did that change my perspective. I learned to appreciate what was happening around me. I was grateful to be alive, grateful Sara made it out of the car wreck, grateful to have shelter, clothes, and food. I also started to appreciate myself. I loved the compassion I had for those in need. I loved how I was so willing to provide for someone who needed help. I never thought that about myself, and started to really admire that part of my character. When I started to love myself and see my own worth, everything changed. I was happier. More content. And more at ease with who I was and the world around me.

Buying shoes used to remind me of being in Disney World. It brought me back to being a giddy kid experiencing magic for the first time. Disney is a wonderland, the happiest place on earth. It's hard to be miserable when you're in the Magic Kingdom. That's how I felt looking at, buying, and wearing fantastic shoes. I felt like trouble did not exist. I felt warm and tingly. I felt like a princess. Though the emotions were fickle and temporary, it was still nice to be wrapped in them at least for a little while. But even Disney World has a closing time.

Today, no material object can take me back to that magical place. Not shoes, clothes, diamonds, or handbags. But I've found that being at peace does. It's more enchanting, soothing, and fulfilling than filling my internal gaping holes with stuff. Knowing I don't have to meet someone else's expectations, knowing I can be myself, and knowing I am free to be me is a feeling like no other. A feeling I've longed for almost twenty years. For the first time in a long time, I was just about there.

Recently, I had the privilege of listening to Terry Bradshaw speak. After talking about football and joking about a variety of topics, he focused on exactly what I am learning. He said that everyone has been put on this earth for a reason and excels at that one thing. God has put in each of us a gift that only we can do best. He reminded the audience that happiness is a material thing that is temporary, but joy lasts forever. Joy is what we need to be striving for and what makes us grateful people. To continually find joy and live it out daily is one of the biggest missions of my life.

9
Looking In and Looking Up

"Faith is the force of life."

~ LEO TOLSTOY

------------◆------------

I have this thing with snowboarding helmets. I love them. It's because one of them saved my life. I had always worn a helmet whenever I took my kids snowboarding by myself, but when Mike went with them, I insisted he wear mine so he wouldn't get hurt. My husband's a little daredevil. Knowing his capacity to push the envelope, particularly while barreling down a steep slope at top speed alongside a bunch of teenagers (that he wants to impress with his athletic skill), I had to make sure his head was protected as much as possible.

A few weeks after I started attending a new church at the end of 2008, our family decided to go snowboarding one Sunday. That morning, I had an overwhelming urge to buy myself a helmet. Since Mike was borrowing mine, I had gone without one for a bit. I had felt safe the few times I had snow-boarded without one, but I felt I was pushing my luck. I needed to buy myself a helmet. The hunch was as strong as the inkling that I had to reconnect with Sherry.

I wasn't quite prepared for the pushy gear salesman I

would meet. When I walked in the store, I stared at the endless rows of helmets, blinded by the wide array of colors. It was like staring at my old sweat suit collection cluttering my tiny closet. Not wanting to spend an arm and a leg on something I was convinced I would never really need, I gravitated to the cheap ones. I mean seriously, what are the chances I was going to take a deadly tumble and knock my head against something or someone? Get real. Those things never happen in real life to real people. You only see them happen in the movies or on some reality TV show where young kids purposely do stupid things.

As soon as I reached out to grab the most inexpensive helmet off the shelf, a salesman's arm jutted out in front of me and tried to push the helmet back in its rightful place.

I was taken back by his rudeness. "Excuse me?" I said with a hint of indignation in my voice.

"Trust me," he assured me. "You don't want to waste your money on that helmet." For the next ten minutes I was given a lecture on safety and headgear and the traumatic injuries that can occur if you hit your head. I groaned. I felt like I was a freshman in high school being instructed on the dangers of weed. The salesman was relentless. I ended up buying the helmet he suggested, the pricey one, just to get him off my back.

The day at the mountain was great. I love spending time with my kids and my husband, feeling the frosty flakes of snow dust my eyelashes and coat my hair, and being energized by the rhythmic pumping of adrenaline coursing through my veins as I cascade down the slopes on my Burton board. There is nothing like hearing the swish of a snowboard beneath your body as you surge down a white shimmery blanket.

Excited to start the day, I got on the ski lift for my first run. As the lift lurched forward giving my body the momentum I needed to hop off, something happened and I fell. I don't know if I lost my balance or just wasn't paying attention, but I slid off the metal contraption for about five feet and then fell backward. It was the weirdest thing. Though my fall was slow and gentle, my head didn't mimic the slow and gentle motion. It snapped back and slammed on the icy ground with such force I felt the wind knocked out of me.

I was in a daze and was blinded by stars spinning in front of my eyes. I could barely make out the background cacophony of concern from people asking if I was all right and the annoying scoff of one of Sara's sarcastic friends, "Good one, Mrs. Reese." I was so out of it, the voices around me sounded slow and distorted, like the scene in the movie *Old School* when Will Ferrell's character shoots himself in the neck with a horse tranquilizer gun and begins his slow descent into unconsciousness.

I was blinking back tears and trying to transition my mind from fog into the present moment, when I was yanked into the present moment by Mike yelling an inch away from my face, "Are you okay, Becky? Are you okay?"

I don't know what it was, but his voice startled me to such a degree I flipped out. I felt like a newborn baby getting jolted out of a peaceful sleep by a Mac truck whizzing by her nursery and honking its obnoxious horn. I yelled at him to go away and got up off the icy ground. I was shaking, unsure of my steps, but I managed to walk down the mountain, dragging my right foot behind me. Still shrouded by the haze of the impact, I talked out loud and encouraged myself to put one foot in front of the other and keep moving forward. I must have been a sight for sore eyes. Curious onlookers stared at me like a freak show as I made my way down the hill. I didn't care who was staring or what they were whispering, though. I was focused on going straight to the lodge to lie down.

I got sick later that night. After spending an hour in tears because I just didn't feel right, I tumbled my way into the bathroom where I stayed all night paying homage to the porcelain king. By the next evening, I'd had enough with feeling sick and nauseous. I called my doctor who told me to drop whatever I was doing and head straight to the hospital. Well, I had to take my girls to gymnastics class and I wasn't about to get the Bad-Mother-of-the-Year award by having them miss their practice, so I waited until they were done rolling and tumbling and dropped them off at home. I drove to the emergency room by myself and found out I had a severe concussion. The admitting physician told me if I hadn't been wearing the helmet, I probably would have died.

Only a week later, actress Natasha Richardson was killed from the same kind of head injury. She fell and hit her head during a ski lesson on a beginner's slope. Though she looked and acted fine immediately afterward, hours later she developed the symptoms of a brain injury and died. Hearing the breaking news reports of her traumatic death shook me to my core. It wasn't like Natasha hit her head when she spiraled out of control down a double black diamond and crashed into a tree; she was merely taking a lesson on the bunny hill. I was emotionally distraught for weeks. It could have been me.

When I went back to the mountain several weeks later, still reeling from my concussion, I spent most of the day in the lodge. The same helmet that saved my life didn't fit anymore and I had no intention of getting on the slopes sans headgear. So while twenty or so young people decked out in vibrant snowboarding garb sipped on steaming cups of hot cocoa and made comments about how sick the slopes were, I examined the plastic piece of equipment and noticed a large crack on the surface. I took it to the pro shop and told them my story, particularly thanking the aggressive salesman who made it his mission to sell me the helmet.

His eyes bugged out when I told him what happened. "Can I borrow it?" he begged, just as insistent as the first time we met. "I want to send it to the manufacturer. We've never seen anything like this before." I was happy to oblige.

To say I feel lucky to be alive is a gross understatement. Even as I write this, I'm getting chills up and down my spine. I believe God taught me a lesson through that fall. I'm on God's time, not mine. God had a plan and His orchestration of that entire day—from us skipping out on church, to placing in me the overpowering hunch to buy a helmet, to interacting with an over-ambitious salesman at the store who wouldn't take "no" to me buying a quality helmet—confirmed that He's got a mission for me. My concussion wasn't a mere accident or an unlucky break. It was a telltale prompting that God was, is, and will always be in control and will continue to lead me down my path of purpose.

That incident revolutionized my spirituality. It brought my faith to another level and even catapulted Mike's personal journey as well. For much of my life, I had attended a local Catholic Church but I never really felt connected to that denomination. There were so many rituals and things I had to do at mass that I didn't understand. Even though I felt peace as I walked through those heavy front doors, I never experienced a sense of belonging or a soul connection. I knew there was more to religion than following rules and regulations, but I wasn't exactly sure what it was.

Add to that, mass was boring. There, I said it. I can't tell you how many times I caught myself staring blankly into space instead of soaking in the message. Don't get me wrong. The Catholic Church is a great institution (though I never got used to the mad hordes of people hightailing it out of the service and practically knocking you over like linebackers to get to the parking lot), I just couldn't see the point of the sermons particularly at my church. They never seemed to apply to my day-to-day life, either by encouraging me in the rat race of life, or providing me with wisdom in handling relationships, or learning about why faith even matters.

Growing up I faithfully attended mass every Sunday. I know my parents had good intentions by taking us there, but the only point I saw was to teach us how to zone out. My parents loved sitting us in the front row which, of course, we kids hated. But rather than whine our way into a spanking, we made our own fun. We'd place bets before the service started on who would fall asleep first listening to the priest in his funky cloak and tiny bifocals towering behind the podium.

When I first got married, I practiced Catholicism to some degree, but as the years passed I slowly drifted away. My kids went to a Catholic school, but they were just going through the motions for the sake of abiding by the school's rules. Mike didn't want anything to do with the Church. He never told me, but I have a feeling something about his upbringing left a sour taste in his mouth and led him to sever all ties to religion.

Kendra, our first nanny, was a Christian. She kept her Bible with her at all times and even read stories from the book to my kids when they were little. I'll be honest. Her religious fanaticism bothered me a bit. I wondered if she was involved in a cult. She invited us to her church many times, but I declined every invitation.

I don't know. Maybe I watched too many nightly specials on bizarre religious sects or something. I did appreciate faith and moral values, but there was no way I was going to be a part of some snake-handling, door-to-door proselytizing, weirdo group. No thank you. Little did I know that West Side Community, the church that would eventually become our spiritual home, was the same church her family been part of since its beginning a few years ago. It was definitely no creepy cult!

Finding a church home couldn't have come at a better time. I was muddling through my days trying to maintain a peaceful home life with the underlying chaos of Stacey's acidic lawsuits and the pile of unpaid bills she left us. Our son Taylor was in middle school and having a rough time. He was getting into fights on almost a daily basis.

One time, a police officer was called in to break up a fight because my son's rage was out of control. Unfortunately, not even a uniformed officer carrying a gun could intimidate or put my son in his place. Taylor gave the cop a disrespectful piece of his mind. Not one of the finest moments for my son and an embarrassing one for his mom.

I was at my wit's end with Taylor. Talking to him did nothing. Neither did disciplining him, grounding him, confiscating his electronic devices, or forbidding him to leave the house except to go to school. His rebellious behavior kept getting worse. We thought the best thing to do would be to surround him with peers who were a better influence. We planted him inside the youth group at West Side Community Church. He loved it. Right away we saw a difference in our son. He was more respectful, listening instead of being defensive and yelling at us, and he was always asking, practically begging, to go to church.

Soon Sara started going with him because two of her friends from school also attended. For a few months they went to Wednesday night youth groups together and even started attending a few Sunday services now and then. Imagine that, my teenage kids going to church without me having to force them to go. Then the unthinkable happened. Sara came up to me one morning and begged me to go to

Sunday service with her.

I didn't want to go. I tried to come up with every excuse in the book. I told her I was too busy taking care of little Madison. I complained that the church was too far away. I even suggested that it might conflict with my Catholic beliefs, even though my faith had gone Rip Van Winkle. I finally relented when Sara was having a bad week and I just knew that having me go with her would make her feel better.

I've got to admit, sitting in a non-Catholic service freaked me out. I was used to the stodginess and flat energy of the conservative church I used to attend. I was used to the only musical component of church being a chanted hymn or a blue-haired lady belting out a chorus a cappella. Sara's church rocked my world. Literally.

There was a band on stage complete with electric guitars and drums. The singers were belting out moving songs that made you want to get up and dance, or for the more conventional like me, clap your hands to the beat. I liked it, but it swept me right out of my comfort zone. I saw this room full of strangers, enjoying and getting into the praise and worship music, some of them were even raising their hands to the sky.

I thought that was odd. Were they stretching? Reaching up for an imaginary object? Asking a question? It was simply a style of worship. We are all free to express ourselves, even in our faith, however we are comfortable. I've found that everyone has their own way of worshiping God. Some close their eyes while they sing or pray. Some clap in adoration. Some lift their hands to the sky. Some don't do anything but stand there. I quickly developed a newfound appreciation for how liberating it is to worship as you see fit. It was quite different from what I was used to.

I enjoyed the sermon that morning. The chubby, balding pastor talked about how he loved running and the feeling of freedom it gave him. Running? Really? My ears perked up and I was immediately drawn to him. I liked his temperament. He was likeable, down-to-earth, and funny. I didn't know church leaders had the ability to make anyone laugh.

When Sara and I walked out of the service, Pastor John Clark pulled us aside and introduced himself. He shook my hand and looked at me straight in the eye. "You were meant to be here this morning," he said.

I politely smiled. I appreciated his warmth but thought, "Yeah, right! You probably say that to everyone new who comes in." (It's hard to break the suspicious habit!)

The third Sunday I attended, Pastor John asked about my husband. I was honest with him and shared how Mike had no intention to have anything to do with church. Mike kept a safe distance from religion and defensively protected those boundaries. Pastor John nodded and said, "Well, I hope to see him at some point. I'd love to meet the father of these fabulous kids." I loved how he didn't make a snide comment or judge my non-church-attending husband.

When I got home, I gave Mike a choice. He could either come to church with us or the church could come to him, meaning I would invite the pastor over for dinner. It wasn't a threat. I just knew in my heart that Mike and Pastor John would get along. They seemed a lot alike. Both have Type A personalities and are sarcastic, motivated, driven, extroverted, and pee-in-your-pants funny. I was convinced they'd be a match made in heaven.

My husband finally visited West Side Community Church a few months later, not long after my snowboarding accident. Much to his chagrin, his mentor had suggested he needed to work on his spiritual side. Needless to say, between his wife hounding him to go to church and his mentor agreeing it was a good idea, he wasn't thrilled. But still, he went.

Mike surprised me that Sunday. Stepping into a church for the first time in seventeen years, guess where he sat. Nope, not the back, not keeping a safe distance between himself and the hoopla. My husband marched right down to the front of the church and plopped down in the first row of chairs. I was shocked. In the best way possible. This was a man who avoided church like the plague. A man who thought Christians were a bunch of fuddy-duddies. A man who always had something better to do with his time, like mowing the lawn or organizing his client folders, than spend an hour of his Sunday morning listening to a sermon.

It was amazing to watch Mike's hesitance transform into enthusiastic participation. After a few weeks, my husband joined a men's group and even planned marketing seminars for entrepreneurs in the church. And get this. He eventually became one of the Pastor's close friends. I was right all along. They were perfect for each other.

It took going there a few times to mentally transition into this new breed of faith, but before I knew it, I had fallen in love with West Side Community. It's our home now. That sense of belonging has nothing to do with the church itself, the cool music, or even the great pastor. It has to do with being in a place that recognizes and teaches about God's partnership with us in life and how we can live each day knowing we have a God-designed destiny. Reactivating my faith in a new way also challenged me to do things that stretched my comfort level.

The biggest missing key to my marriage was spirituality. Mike and I both believed in the spiritual side of things. We each understood how important it is to be a balanced and purposeful individual, but we didn't know how to get to that place of growth. My husband had devoted his entire being to work and sensed that faith could be the link to even out his priorities. I felt incomplete and was struggling with the demise of my friendship with Stacey. Good things happened when we finally took the leap into faith.

I encountered a faith that was personal. Real. Deep. I wasn't just being entertained by hearing Bible stories preached on Sunday; I was starting to see them come alive in my life. For the first time I witnessed the power of God working in me. When I started reading the Bible, I was amazed at how many of the stories I had heard about in Catholic children's classes related to my modern-day life, like David and Goliath, for instance.

David was a puny teenager God chose to battle the formidable Goliath, a Philistine giant known for his brawn and his deadly strength. When David prepared to face the menacing Godzilla, King Saul suited him with metal armor and weapons that weighed practically as much as the little guy. David quickly realized he would be at a disadvantage with the extra bulk and made the jaw-dropping decision to fight Goliath with his slingshot and a few stones. That's it. He didn't have backup or a state-of-the-art defense system. There were no armed guards behind him. No AK47 over his shoulder. No machete on his belt. David had nothing to beat this giant except an elastic band and a few large pebbles.

David stood with the Israelite army at the top of a hill while Goliath beat on his chest in the valley below, spewing violent threats at the underdog. David had to walk down the hill to meet his challenger. It was probably the longest walk of his life, especially because the future king didn't rush. He took his time and even spent a few minutes picking out the perfect stones with which to crush his enemy. He didn't panic. He didn't cry. He didn't stay at the top of the hill where it was safe and where he was protected by his nation's army.

When I recently read that story, I was reminded of my own life and having to face giants like my miscarriage, the ugly battle between Mike and Stacey, the conflicts in my own family and those with my mother. It challenged me to think about how I handle battles. When tough times come—when my insecurities want to come out and party and doubt attacks my peace—do I stay in that place where it's comfortable yet deadly? Or do I venture out into the valley to fight those enemies? Do I rush into battles, panicking the entire way, or do I allow the Lord to calmly lead me? Am I as strong and confident as David was, knowing that even though his adversary had the human strength and fortitude to pummel him to bits and pieces, God was on his side and that's all it takes to win?

∞

So many things have changed since I started focusing on building up my spiritual muscles. Even my giving has been reformed. I'm grateful for the opportunity to work with other people in the church to serve the community, not just orchestrate my own giving program. West Side offered me the chance to serve in a way I hadn't before, like volunteering to deliver turkeys at Thanksgiving to families who were in need.

I took my two oldest children to a seedy neighborhood that honestly I hoped never to set foot in again. We walked up to the trailer where the family was living and a slew of questions ran through my head. What if we get shot? What if my kids are bitten by a mean-looking pit bull? What if we get carjacked? When we knocked on the door, my heart was pounding in my chest and my palms were sweating from the machine-gun succession of what-if questions that weighed on my mind.

When the door opened and my children and I offered this family a turkey, my fears melted away and the angst was replaced by compassion. These beautiful people were so grateful for the kind, albeit small, token of thoughtfulness. It made me grateful for everything I had and reminded me that fears have no place when it comes to serving others.

Donating our time and money had always come easily for Mike and me. When our faith began to grow, however, our giving took on a whole new meaning. Reading *The Four Spiritual Laws of Prosperity* gave me something new to chew on, the concept of tithing. In the past, I was more than happy to drop a couple of bucks into the offering plate at church, but I never considered regularly giving my money to a place where I was spiritually fed. I was curious about this spiritual principle and had a lot of questions. How much should I tithe? Was that amount before or after taxes or before or after we covered payroll?

When I talked to my pastor about it, he explained it in layman's terms and encouraged us to test it. Pastor John mimicked God's dare in Malachi 3:10 when He told His people, "Bring all the tithes into the storehouse so there will be enough food in my Temple. If you do," says the Lord of Heaven's Armies, "I will open the windows of heaven for you. I will pour out a blessing so great you won't have enough room to take it in! Try it! Put me to the test!"

Pastor John told us, "Try it for three months. If you don't see a dramatic difference in your finances, I will refund your money." That was a pretty lofty guarantee, and the risk involved made my husband itch to take up the challenge, God and Pastor John's. I wrote a check on Sunday for the ten percent of the income that had come in that week. The problem was, we didn't have any money left to cover the amount. I dropped the check in the offering bucket out of sheer faith.

I called our bookkeeper on Monday and blankly told her, "I just wrote a $5,000 check. Please make sure we have enough money to cover it." Now, where that money was going to come from, I hadn't a clue. It was a total gamble on my part, but I figured if tithing was a way to thank God for His provision and teach us about the laws of sowing of reaping, it would work out. If not, I'd know for sure the whole thing was a hoax.

Only an hour later, a deposit came in the mail for just under $5,000. We had sufficient funds to cover my tithe check. I was in shock. Even though I knew God could do it—that fraction of belief is, after all, what prompted me to step out in faith in the first place; I was astonished when it actually came to pass. I thought, "Oh my goodness. This works. It really works!" I've learned that God is faithful and He always knows what He's doing. He doesn't need our help, our guidance, our suggestions, or our knowledge of the back way. Without fail, He puts to shame the best human planners and control-freaks. I know. I'm one of them.

❦

When I had the snowboarding incident and felt God speaking in my heart that my life had a purpose, I discovered a new peace of mind. I now rest my faith and confidence in Him when I'm not sure what direction I should go, when I question if what I do or think matters, and when bad things happen outside of our control.

My assistant recently had a miscarriage. She had been trying to have a baby for a few years and was ecstatic when she found out she was pregnant. A few weeks later, the baby died.

My heart broke for her. Partly because I, too, had gone through a miscarriage, but mostly because I could feel her pain and wanted desperately to take it away. I know that telling her God has His way and purpose even in senseless tragedies would not provide her with immediate consolation; it can come off as such a tiring cliché sometimes, but there is truth to the statement. Eventually, one can see that truth as it is slowly revealed.

God never gives us anything we can't handle. The Bible tells us that God's grace is sufficient for us (2 Corinthians 12:9). That means if we go through illness, He will give us His grace to see us through. If we fall into temptation, He will give us His grace to run the other way. If we get sick, He will give us His grace to endure the trial. If we are on the verge of divorce, He will give us His grace to deal with the situation.

I think about losing my baby, and while it still makes me sad whenever I talk about it, I realize that if the little one had lived, I might not have had Madison. I might not have had that big age gap between my children that brought with it the chance for my older kids to care for, influence, and watch Madison grow. Sara and Madison are so close because Sara feels an enormous desire to care for her little sister. It's a beautiful thing to watch in action.

Living a life of faith is never easy. There is no road to perfection in Christianity. You don't wake up one day and enter into a magical life where you walk around with an invisible halo above your head. Sometimes it's not easy to do the right thing. Staying connected with God, which is a crucial element to the Christian faith, requires you to live on purpose each day. Purposefully communing with your Creator. Purposefully seeking Him. Purposefully living out Biblical principles. It doesn't come naturally to most people, me included.

I've realized the more I strengthen my commitment to

God, the more changes I see and the more fulfilled I feel, even in spite of hardships. I'll admit I get distracted easily. And I'm just plain busy. There are times I find it challenging, nearly impossible, to set aside a few minutes during the day or, sadly, even a week to slow down and rest in God's presence.

But you know what happens like clockwork? I'll get a wakeup call to remind me I need to get back on the spiritual tracks. I'm seeking God but find myself doubting Him. Sometimes I feel distant from Him, especially when I get caught up doing a million things.

Recently, Pastor John started a 12-week series on the famous David and Goliath Bible story. I missed two Sundays in a row because I was traveling, but was able to attend a service right before a trip to Las Vegas to attend a conference. On that Sunday, the Pastor spent the entire message dissecting just two verses in that text.

On the flight to Vegas, I opened a book I was reading to a random page and my finger fell on the author's perspective on not only the David and Goliath story, but on the same verses my pastor had explored the day before. Was it chance? Happenstance? Life? I believe it was God showing me something since the Scripture passage had to do with how God chose David for a specific purpose.

At the conference, I continued to see sign after sign that God was speaking to me through that truth. He had a special plan for me, something I would have never dreamed on my own. I felt an inner call to express myself with pen and paper and talk about my struggles so others could be encouraged in their own journey, the idea that I had only half–seriously toyed with some time ago but kept knocking on the door of my heart.

The more I grow spiritually, the bigger the desire in me to learn more and the more I can see God working in mysterious ways. It's a beautiful cycle. I've grown more comfortable in my faith, realizing that just because I'm a Christian doesn't mean I'll become a poster child for faith overnight. There are pieces of myself that have drastically improved and areas that are still under construction. My pastor has helped me see that I can live through Christ and still be human. The point of needing Him is because we are growing and falling and getting back up and taking a step forward and two steps back every now and again.

The life of faith is a journey. It takes time. It takes effort. It takes desire. There are no overnight successes, just changed lives.

10
The Art of Self-Care

"Sometimes the dreams that come true are the dreams
you never even knew you had."
~ Alice Sebold

$\mathscr{I}$ think if a lot of women started taking care of them-selves as well as they take care of their families, they'd be in a lot better shape. I'm not talking about just physical shape. I'm talking about feeling fulfilled emotionally, mentally, spiritually and yes, of course, physically. Most women do a great job of feeling tired, overworked, and stressed. This is especially true for a mom who is running around cleaning spit-up, taking this one to soccer practice and that one to a play date, keeping the house at least semi-orderly and clean, and maybe even spending a few days working outside the home.

But not all stressed out women are moms. There's the on-the-go woman who has prioritized her career over her health or the single person who is known as the go-to gal in her family, the one whom everyone calls when they need help or a favor because they know she'll always say yes. Either way, most women struggle with taking care of themselves. If you can relate, you might be in the same place I was years ago, not knowing where to begin or how to take care of myself. Taking care of yourself might even seem like a selfish thing to do. Or time consuming. Or a waste of your precious time. Trust me, it's none of those things.

Recently I flew out to Los Angeles for a photo shoot at the suggestion and orchestration of my coach Tamara. It was an eye-opening experience that made me appreciate the importance of self-care and evidenced how far I have come in that department. Yes, there was a lot of glamour, hair, and makeup. Fancy clothes were involved in the process, too, but what I learned from that shoot didn't have anything to do with vanity. It had to do with satisfying a part of myself that still yearned to feel beautiful. By now you know how, for a long time, I neglected my appearance in many ways, thinking I wasn't worthy or good enough to feel pretty. But as I stood in the stark white studio surrounded by intimidating lighting equipment and being directed by a photographer who snapped away while making me laugh, I understood once again—because sometimes we have to be continually reminded of certain things in order to get it—that it is part of a woman's nature to want to twirl and radiate and shine like the beautiful gems that we are. It's not shallow. It's just who we are. We all want to feel pretty.

On the day I was scheduled to leave for California, the weather reports were grim. Forecasters predicted snow and lots of it. I checked the website for my tiny airport every fifteen minutes to see what flights were canceled, which were grounded, and which weren't coming in. After wanting to pull my hair out from my obsessive behavior that wasn't doing me a lick of good, I put on my favorite pair of high heels and headed to the airport. City of Angels, here I come.

My flight was canceled. I hobbled back out the terminal and into my truck where my husband was patiently waiting for me behind the driver's seat. All three inches of my heels were covered in snow. I roughly wrapped my arms around my jacket-free body, feeling silly that I'd opted not to don a coat in hopes I'd reach L.A. in only a couple of hours. I was cold, wet, and disappointed.

I didn't stay annoyed for long. The rebooking process was seamless. Everything, including my hotel visit and the shoot, was pushed back to the following day. In the midst of rescheduling, I was struck by a mind shift. This trip was going to be so much more than getting some professional snapshots. I just knew it. Something was happening that I couldn't see or put my finger on. God was working divine magic.

Later that day, something nudged me to change my flight to a later one. I did, only to find out my brother had been stuck in Michigan for a few days because of the snow and had been rescheduled to fly out on the same outgoing flight. To my delight, we would be flying together. I could almost hear God chuckle. It was a welcome divine-ordained happenstance. On the plane ride to Detroit, my first layover, my brother and I had hours to catch up, hours that we normally didn't have together.

Sunny Los Angeles was a welcome respite from the hurricane of white I left behind in Traverse City. Once I checked myself into the hotel, I headed straight for the enormous tub that was beckoning my name. I slid into the oversized porcelain masterpiece and immersed myself in a thick and luxurious layer of bubbles that smelled like a lavender garden. I closed my eyes and thought about my life and how far I had come. I wasn't as afraid as I used to be. I wasn't as insecure. I wasn't tied down by the expectations of others. I was finally putting myself ahead of the class for the first time.

Most importantly, I believed in myself. I knew I was created for more than indulging in anxiety and self-doubt. I was created to stand and live in confidence as a daughter of God. Instead of worrying about the photo shoot the next day and whether the camera would flatter my figure, complexion, or hair, I rested in the knowledge of my change. I rested in peace. Let me tell you something, it was a very good feeling.

I woke very early the next day and got ready for my hair appointment. I wondered what these fabulous stylists were going to do to my tresses. Cut it? Reshape it? Throw on an intense color? As I stepped off the elevator and headed to the salon, which happened to be in the hotel lobby, I was amazed by how beautiful the women of Los Angeles are. Tall, thin, impeccably dressed and sporting fabulous flowing manes, these goddesses added eye candy to the already exquisite décor of the posh hotel. But I didn't feel jealous or less than them because I didn't look like them. I simply admired their beauty and confidently click-clacked my way down the marble hall wearing the same heels that had been grounded in Michigan snow a day earlier.

What struck me about the salon wasn't just how very Hollywood chic everything was, from the funky-looking stylists dressed in all black, to the chocolate and cream cushioned chairs, to the lavish outdoor patio, to the exotic flowers casting off their vibrant colors and fragrance. It was how most of the customers were hovering over their phones. You could barely hear a peep out of them. Just a grunt of an acknowledgement to their stylist that they liked how their hair looked. Other than that, these people were buried in texting, messaging, and scheduling their calendars. I found it a bit rude and somewhat sad. Could technology be pushing us toward a lonelier world?

I shoved my phone into the bottomless pit of my big purse. I wanted to soak in the moment, not be enslaved by the distractions of missed calls or emails that I used to think took precedence over "me" time. As a matter of fact, for most of the day I kept my hands away from my phone, making a statement that this day was mine. It was not owned by people who thought silly things were emergencies that required my special skills to fix, solve, or repair. No more. It was time to do something I wanted, undisturbed.

My stylist was fantastic. His down-to-earth demeanor and genuine compliments reignited the mind shift I had experienced when my first flight to L.A. was canceled. We talked about the work I was doing with Tamara while he fussed with my hair and combed it in all sorts of strange ways to capture a particular vision in his mind. As I started a lengthy monologue of the outside changes I wanted to make to feel more beautiful, he abruptly stopped.

With one hand holding a lock of my hair in his hand so it was parallel with the floor, he said, "Becky, you are so beautiful. You don't need to change a thing. When Tamara told me your story...." His face fell and he was silent for a few seconds. "Well, I just wish you could have met my mom. She really needed to hear what you have to say."

I almost gushed a Niagara Falls of tears. I can't tell you how wonderful his assurances were. Don't get me wrong. I didn't need his string of compliments that I was beautiful, courageous, or special in order to convince myself of those things. I wasn't feeding on his affirmation like a starved animal. It was just soothing to hear. And encouraging. And sure, it did make me feel good.

I entered into another mind shift as this man artistically and effortlessly snipped away at my locks. Something clicked. I knew exactly what my purpose was, to empower other women, especially moms, to learn the art of self-care. I wanted to help them not to forget about themselves as the years fly by. Not to hoist the world onto their shoulders and spend the rest of their lives carrying unnecessary burdens. Not to focus on everyone and everything else except their own selves. It's no secret that when we are nourishing our inner and outer natures, we are better mothers, better wives, better girlfriends, better daughters, better executives, better entrepreneurs, and better people.

After hugging my stylist and remarking on the fabulous job he did with my hair and how he made my salon experience memorable and heart-warming, I hopped into a cab. It was time to do a little retail therapy to celebrate my progress. "Beverly and Robertson, please," I told the driver. Though not as well known as the famous Rodeo Drive, this section of Tinsel Town is famous for glitzy stores where celebrities frequently shop.

My cab driver refused my request. "No," he said in broken English. "Too expensive. How 'bout more cheap place?"

I felt like I was on the *Amazing Race*, telling some guy to take me somewhere I needed to go but being met with resistance and having a wedge driven into my strategic plans. I said, this time more sternly, "Beverly and Robertson, sir."

He sighed, shook his head, and clicked on the meter, muttering unintelligibly under his breath. I was so pissed on the way there. Who was this random man to decide where I should or should not go shopping? Who was he to decide whether shopping place X was too expensive for me? Who was he to make a decision for me that I had already made on my own? It was another mind shift. I make the rules, buddy, not you or anyone else.

I gave the driver his due and strutted onto the sidewalk. I walked straight into Chanel where I came out a few minutes later with a bag holding a gorgeous pair of black pumps. I was still fuming at the cab driver. *See?* I thought. *I can shop wherever I want to shop.*

While I didn't see any movie stars in the stores where I

trickled in and out, I did bump into one on the sidewalk. Actually, bump is a loose term. I wasn't paying attention, neither was he for that matter, and I tripped on a crack in the concrete, falling forward, straight into him. Not one of my most graceful moments. I was petrified that in a matter of a few seconds I would be blinded by paparazzi cameras and a news-breaking report would flash on TMZ, "Klutzy pedestrian crashes into celebrity X." But that didn't happen. We smiled, parted ways, and I headed back to the hotel.

I felt like the Grinch who stole Christmas. My heart grew three sizes that day. I was finally alive to the fact that I loved myself. I was accepting, respecting, and appreciating every part of me, no changes necessary. I was finally radiating the inner confidence, calm, and peace I had been searching for my entire life. I can't say I've fully arrived, because let's be honest, none of us actually officially arrive anywhere in this life. There is always somewhere to go, but my inner being was finally being charged with power, life, and joy. It was a destination that at some painful moments in my life I thought I would never reach. The revealing day prompted another soak in the tub.

The day of the photo shoot brought about a different type of anxiety. I'd never had a professional photo shoot besides the obligatory Christmas family portrait taken at Sears. This was a whole new arena. My photographer, Lesley Bohm, works with famous soap opera stars, actresses, and musicians and here she was, shooting a mother of five kids from a small town in Michigan.

When the stylists came on set to apply my makeup and touch up my hair from the day before, I sat in the chair and submitted to their brushes, color choices, and tools meant to bring out my natural beauty. I felt like a princess. It sounds like such a meaningless platitude, doesn't it? But it was true. I felt like a little girl twirling in a fairy princess costume in front of my parents and showing off how marvelous I looked. I can't remember the last time I felt like that, unencumbered by self-consciousness and empowered by a sense of inner and outer beauty.

At first, I felt like a clodhopper in front of the camera because I was so nervous. My face twitched from smiling too much. I laughed at inappropriate times. I felt stiff and the first couple of poses felt unnatural and awkward, like picture day at school. But it didn't take long for my confidence to take up root, thanks to Lesley's effortless promptings. She could sense my nervousness and started cracking jokes to loosen me up. It worked. She snapped away while we talked about life, fashion, and juicy celebrity gossip.

When I saw the pictures, I almost passed out. They were amazing. I thought, "Oh my god. This is really me. Really. And I'm beautiful." How strange that I was never able to notice my beauty in such a telling way before. It wasn't just my polished look that made for a great shoot. My inner confidence was busting through and was easily visible through the frames. My eyes were lit up like the Macy's fireworks display. There was life in them. Passion. Purpose. Peace. I looked exactly how I felt, truly happy.

High off that feeling of ecstasy, I thought about my snow-boarding accident. I'm convinced I should have died that day. I should not be here today writing this book. But for some reason, God had other plans and He was going to finish the good work He started in me. I believe He wanted to show me the world of women out there who are in the same boat that I once was, bobbing about a dark sea on a ragtag mesh of hastily tied together wooden planks, feeling lost, dumpy and frumpy, sad, depressed, lonely, anxious, and afraid.

It's a very real and a very hopeless place. Even though it

wields a magnetic pull, we can abandon ship and pull ourselves safely to shore. We don't have to spend our lives feeling out of sorts. We can feel purposeful, beautiful, joyful, content, fulfilled, peaceful, and confident. Believe me, I know. I've had that about-face and living life this way has proved more exciting and gratifying than I could ever have imagined.

Let me give you a piece of advice. Sometimes when we experience moments of victory in our journeys, we desperately want those we love to share the joys with us. Sometimes they will, but sometimes they won't. If they won't, give them the benefit of the doubt. Don't assume they are bad, selfish, or uncaring people; maybe they just don't understand.

I had to learn that I could still celebrate me even though, let's say, my husband didn't match my enthusiasm or give me the response I expected of him. Because guess what? It's not about him. It's about me. Sometimes it is about me, you, and us. We don't take care of ourselves so others can take notice. We don't take care of ourselves so we can show the world how extraordinary we are. We don't take care of ourselves to get praise, accolades, or a good old-fashioned pat on the back. We take care of ourselves because it's the right thing to do for our well-being and it makes us better people.

I remember coming home from my trip and anticipating having Mike waiting up for me. I had a late flight coming into Michigan, but I knew he was always up until the wee hours of the morning either working or playing poker. Why wouldn't he stay up for his wife who had been away for a couple of days? I couldn't wait to tell him about my experience, about how gorgeous I looked and felt, about the handful of a-ha! moments I had, about how this trip was evidence that I had really evolved.

But he was asleep. Sound asleep. Loudly snoring. Didn't even budge an inch despite the racket I purposely made unpacking my suitcase and throwing my toiletries back on the dresser. It frustrated me. It shouldn't have, but it did. I was so proud of myself and felt a twinge of bitterness that the man I had pledged to spend the rest of my life with and with whom I had five children couldn't even keep his eyes open until a little after midnight. It's not like he was oblivious to how pivotal this trip was for me. He knew how important this photo shoot was, all right, and he had the nerve to choose zzz's over me?

Hemming, hawing and pouting, I went downstairs and started pounding away at my laptop to journal my thoughts. While I initially felt the aftershocks of disappointment, I realized that it didn't matter if Mike was asleep or not. I had those moments. I had those epiphanies. I had an amazing time. I had fun. And I had the power not to let anyone, not even my husband whom I adore so much, rob me from my moment. If you are starting out on your journey of self-care, do your best to ignore the naysayers or those around you who are negative or who don't notice. Remember that you are the best. You are beautiful. Don't you ever forget it.

☙

I'm sure many of you wish you had learned the lessons of your later years earlier on, but that's what happens in life. We gain our insight after we go through challenging times, but we can use it to better ourselves from that moment forward and to share our wisdom with others so they don't make the same mistakes we've made.

That's how I feel when I look at the exhausted mother in the grocery store trying to navigate the grocery cart with her two kids clinging to her jacket and a newborn screaming at the top of her lungs. I know where she's been and how she's feeling. I think about the woman who has poured her young life into her husband and children only to find herself divorced at forty with two grown children who are doing their own thing. I know how empty she feels, void of purpose or direction. I think about the young lady who because she has her ducks in row is the one her family depends on for emotional, financial, and physical support. I know how weary she feels and how often she asks herself, "What about me?"

I want others to know that it's possible to get out of the ruts in which we can easily find ourselves and into the life that we've always longed for. A few months ago, I came up with a list I had typed on my Blackberry (I had made the switch from my trusty iPhone because I would end up butt-dialing random people all day). This list was nothing like the list of complaints I had jotted down at the beginning of my journey. My new list is special. It's what has helped me regain control of my life and given me my life back.

For starters, the number one thing to practice is self-care. It's essential. It's become my foundational premise. I like to think of self-care as loving yourself like no one else has loved you, and then multiplying that love by ten. We only get one life. There are no do-overs. Sure, you can get plastic surgery to fix up body parts you don't like, but you can't get a new heart or soul because yours is tired, worn-out, stressed, or sad.

Because we are unique and have different needs, self-care looks different from woman to woman. You might enjoy taking a bubble bath every night or treating yourself to a spa treatment once a month. You might want to take a continuing education class or workshop. Or start an exercise program. Or learn a new language. Or have ten minutes of quiet time a day. Or journal. Or get a new haircut or color. Or give your wardrobe a makeover and get rid of the clothes that don't flatter you anymore. Or get a free makeup lesson at my favorite store in the world, Sephora. Or learn a new hobby. Did I give you enough ideas yet?

Whatever it is that helps you to feel balanced, energized, content, and full of joy is a stepping stone to taking care of yourself the way God intended. I believe that's a part of what Jesus meant when He told us that He came so that we could live an abundant life (John 10:10). An abundant life is not necessarily trouble free; it's about feeling whole and having a peaceful inner core in the midst of trouble.

You know what else self-care is? It's not just doing or buying something. It's about changing our mentality. It's refusing to be driven by fears, accepting life as it comes one day at a time, and trusting your instincts. Through therapy, I've learned to heed my gut calls. I'm a highly sensitive person and a pretty good judge of character. I've taken this innate skill and applied it to decision-making, no longer letting fears or self-doubt dominate my choices. Now I better trust myself in the driver's seat.

Two, get healthy. I'm not talking about getting thin. I'm talking about focusing your attention on your health so you can feel better, have more energy, and enjoy life more. I focus on eating the right foods and exercising for only twenty minutes every day. I don't care how busy you are, I'm sure you can squeeze in less than a half hour of daily activity. My trainer has me doing full body exercises like squats, lunges, and pushups. And boy, even though it may not seem like a lot of time, they are challenging and they do work.

Three, get a grip on your finances. Empower yourself so you can feel secure with your own money. Stop spending and start saving. Just by putting away as little as a dollar a day, in one year you can save almost $400. What if instead of buying your daily latte or breakfast sandwich, you put away $2 or even $5 a day? That's a lot of money saved without it hurting your wallet. It feels great when you can contribute to your family's finances by being a good steward of your money and socking away extra cash for a vacation or even as security for your family. I know, I have experience.

Four, nourish your spiritual connection. I believe God has made each and everyone of us unique and special just the way we are. He has given me purpose, and finding my spirituality and developing a personal relationship with Him was the turning point of my life.

I need to be careful what I'm feeding myself spiritually. In order for me to live an authentic spiritual life, I have to be sure what I'm doing or thinking about helps not hinders my growth. Am I hanging out with people who are a good influence on me? Am I watching TV shows that will help me to be more like the person I aim to be? Am I focusing on material things that are keeping my gaze off of God? These are good questions to ask.

I like the Bible verse that says God "rewards those who sincerely seek Him" (Hebrews 11:6). To be able to make God a daily part of my life is a blessing. I am overwhelmed with gratitude for my family, for our health, and for the opportunity we have to connect with Him on such a personal level. Find your spiritual connection and live life taking steps to grow that connection stronger. When we have a spiritual connection, it is only then that true freedom, soul freedom, can be ushered in.

Five, spice up your relationship with your significant other. Don't rely on your partner to pull out all the romantic stops. Take control of the situation yourself. It's easy to let the spark wane when you've been married for a while. But even if time, children, and life stresses have put a distance between you and your spouse, remember the reason you fell in love with them in the first place. Ignite that spark when you can.

I'm guilty as sin in this department because I allowed my exhaustion, the kids, and a myriad of excuses to keep me from caring for the sensual side of my marriage. I can tell you there is a big difference when we nurture the needs of our husbands. Know what else? They become better husbands when we do this!

Six, find your passion. Create a commitment to do something that makes you happy, whether it's volunteering at your local shelter, starting a small group Bible study in your neighborhood, or even writing a book.

Seven, embrace change. If there is one constant in life besides death and taxes, it's change. Since it's inevitable, you might as well stop looking at it in the negative. Instead of being paralyzed by fear, learn to adapt when a shift happens and do the best that you can in that situation. It might be a job change, an illness in the family, a move to a new town, an addition to the family, or financial upheaval. Whatever it is, move through change with a positive attitude and watch how you grow stronger and wiser from the experience.

Looking back, it's been a wild ride. From being a small-town girl who pinched pennies to having an abundance of financial resources. From being broke to being a millionaire's wife with a summer home. From drowning in insecurity, discontent, and emotional unrest to enjoying life, learning balance, and ultimately finding peace, passion, and purpose. It took me a long time to get where I am but it was worth every step.

You may be thinking of taking steps toward inner peace in your world of chaos or you could already be on that path. It's not easy, but I want to encourage you. Sure, you will stumble along the way. In fact, there will be times where you want to quit because it is just plain easier to remain comfortable in your misery than feel stretched by growing pains. When those moments come, remember they will pass and you know what else? They're good for us. They help to propel us forward. It's like what M. Scott Peck said, "The truth is that our finest moments are most likely to occur when we are feeling deeply uncomfortable, unhappy, or unfulfilled. For it is only in such moments, propelled by our discomfort, that we are likely to step out of our ruts and start searching for different ways or truer answers."

Oh how I miss the innocent and carefree days of childhood. Ever stop to watch kids play? Whether they're throwing a Frisbee at the park, hanging on the bars of a jungle gym, or bouncing around at Chuck E. Cheese, they all have this in common—they play hard and are full of giggles, smiles, and belly laughs. When they learn to ride a bike for the first time, the joy on their face is indescribable. The first time they stand at home plate and hit a pitched baseball, they exude contagious enthusiasm. There are many days where I wish I could be a child like that, playing without a care in the world and producing such a positive energy.

But here's the thing. I can't be that child because I'm an adult with a husband, children, and life responsibilities. And it's okay! For me, playing like a carefree little girl is the equivalent of living in every moment I am given, enjoying the company of whom I'm with at the time, and engaging with my husband when we chat minutes before we both fall asleep. I don't let fears, self-doubt, insecurity and guilt plague me anymore. I look forward to learning more, growing, and best of all, leaving a mark on the world.

Can you hear my wings flapping?

About the Author

Becky Reese is an author, entrepreneur, and philanthropist who values the importance of family, and believes that all women should feel beautiful. Her Millionaire Mom Makeover event set for January, 2012, will transform a few women the same way she went through her journey. Her brand new clothing line, debuting in the Spring of 2012, will feature functional and fashionable sports clothes for women of all sizes and shapes, and her Sexy Moms Running Club, launched in Summer 2011, aims at bringing women together through running.

Becky is dedicated to helping families, especially children, in need throughout her church and community. She lives in Northern Michigan with her husband Mike of nineteen years, and their five children.

For more information and to interact, visit Becky's websites BeckyReese.com and marriedtoamillionairebook.com.

Smartly published™ through the

Smart Women's Institute
of Entrepreneurial Learning

Imprint Publishing Program

in collaboration with

Wyatt-MacKenzie Publishing
DEADWOOD, OREGON

*For more details on how to
publish the Smart Way:*

www.smartwomeninstitute.com/publishimprint

CPSIA information can be obtained at www.ICGtesting.com
Printed in the USA
LVOW061840070212

267543LV00008B/3/P